THE
OIL-PROTEIN
DIET
COOKBOOK

Dr. Johanna Budwig

Apple Publishing Co. Ltd.
220 E. 59th Ave. • Vancouver • B.C • Canada • V5X 1X9 • Tel.(604) 325-2888

ISBN:0-9695272-2-5

CONTENTS

PREFACE

Originally written in German, this unique "cookbook" was founded upon scientific principles encompassing physics and medicine. Therefore, much care and attention was necessary in translating this very important work for the benefit of layperson and professional alike.

Dr. Budwig _ scientist, author and lecturer, has spent more than half of her 85 years explaining her simple truth to the world _ *how highly unsaturated essential fatty acids (like those found in flax oil), when combined with high quality protein (which makes essential fats easily soluble), will counteract toxic and poisonous accumulations in all tissue.*

Her flair in preparing food is an extension of her scientific discoveries and will inspire many as they get a sense of this amazing woman's enthusiasm - her zest for life. The very young and not so young _ the athlete as well as the convalescing _ will benefit greatly by adhering to the simple regimens outlined within these pages.

Hippocrates wrote, "...let food be your medicine!"
...Dr. Budwig shows us how!

Alexander Pazitch/Publisher

OLEOLOX-FAT

Note: This is referred to often throughout this book and is Fat to be used as a spread on bread, vegetables, buckwheat, rice, etc.(or in soup).

Ingredients:

250g coconut fat,
1 onion,
10 garlic cloves,
125 ccm Flax Seed Oil.

10 garlic cloves

1 onion

250g coconut fat

heat 3 minutes
strain into:

Flax oil 125ccm

Preparation:

Cut 1 medium sized onion in half and brown slightly in 250g of heated (100ºC) coconut fat. Cook for approximately 15 min., add 10 garlic cloves and heat for additional *3 minutes only*. Strain the fat through a sieve into 125ccm of Flax Seed Oil (previously chilled for 1/2 hour in the freezer) Keep this mixture refrigerated and bring to the table in small portions as required.

Note: As a rule, Flax Oil and OLEOLOX should never be heated. If you prepare sauces according to my recipes, the sensitive, unsaturated fatty acids of Flax Oil are somewhat protected by the sulfhydryl group of spices (eg: pepper). Be careful not to heat the OLEOLOX more than one minute.

INTRODUCTION

My experience in counselling patients led me to the following conclusion: it is no longer sufficient today to simply advise people to avoid harmful fats and chemical preservatives in food _ instead I advise them to adhere as close to nature as possible when choosing fats, fruits, vegetables and cereals. Viewed objectively, this advice should help even the seriously ill cancer patient regain his/her health. Unfortunately, however, the homemakers of our day have a weak command of the culinary arts. Knowledge of spices is retained principally by the butcher, while the homemaker is at best, familiar with salt, pepper, chives and parsley. Cooking with the aforementioned herbs and spices, the homemaker is unable to enhance the flavor of the food without adding "ready-made products" such as bouillon cubes or meat products. It is much more pleasant for the whole family, if the homemaker understands how to give his/her cooking that personal touch. The cooking methods should increase the family's pleasure of being at home. Receiving superior foods at home will soon tire you of restaurant cooking that makes use of wrong and overheated fat.

The correct choice and use of fats is extremely important for the whole family, affecting even their emotional well being. This cookbook, "THE OIL-PROTEIN DIET" presents a model of nutrition by restricting itself to optimal foods.

This cookbook is designed to help not only the ailing, but also those wishing to assist the unwell in their recovery.

OIL, THE VITAL INGREDIENT OF OUR TIME

Flax Seed Oil has always been capable of performing miracles. Fats regulate the entire metabolic system and the production of energy and of new cells, more than any other nutriment.

The basis for the entire utilization of nutriments is destroyed, when highly active, natural fats are replaced by fatty substances that have been artificially altered, devitalized and stabilized against oxidation. Such blocking substances in the organism are the leading cause of most diseases we see today. Help is available in the form of highly active nutritional fats, found in their optimal form in Flax Seed Oil and corresponding spreads. It is important to properly balance fats with protein _ the Oil-Protein Diet.

GENERAL INFORMATION ON DIETS FOR THE UNWELL

Within the framework of the Oil-Protein Diet for the unwell, a glass of sauerkraut juice is recommended in the morning and in the evening. Drinking freshly pressed vegetable and fruit juices throughout the day is also recommended. Concerning fruit juices, only pure and natural juices (without added sugar) should be selected. Avoid the sweet ciders.

Firstly, it is essential that the unwell and diabetics alike consume the permitted amount of Flax Seed Oil or "OLEOLOX"* Later, a wheat-germ oil regimen can be added and a small glass of wine is always allowed.

This diet offers complete nutrition and is especially recommended in preparation for physical exertion (ie: for athletes).

---

* See page (vii) for illustration on preparing "OLEOLOX-FAT" at home.

BREAKFAST (FOR THE UNWELL)

For breakfast, a Muesli should be consumed regularly. Put two tablespoons of LINOMEL* in a glass dish. Cover this with fresh fruit in season, (ie: berries, cherries, apricots, peaches, grated apples or fruit salad). Then prepare the cream with Quark and Flax Seed Oil. Flavor with nuts, lemon juice, bananas**, (See No. 1 to No. 16). This cream is put over the fruit as one would apply whipped cream. Then garnish with nuts, fruits, raisins, shredded coconut, etc. As a spread on bread, only OLEOLOX should be used (butter and margarine are not acceptable). Before noon, the heavy eater is allowed all types of cheeses with radishes, tomatoes, cucumber slices, etc. Those who relish goose-fat with hard cheese will also enjoy OLEOLOX with hard cheese. Herb teas can serve as beverages, and the occasional cup of black tea is also permitted.

LUNCH (FOR THE UNWELL)

The midday meal should not include any meat. A raw vegetable salad is recommended as an appetizer. For oil, use either Flax Seed Oil on its own, or in companion with pumpkin seed oil. (The use of what is termed "salad oil" is strictly forbidden.) All types of lettuce may be used for the salad platter, as well as grated tubers, carrots, kohlrabi, radishes, comfrey root, etc. It is important that the raw-food dish be eaten as an appetizer. (see recipes No. 57-77, especially No. 70).

For dessert, one can serve a Quark/Flax Seed Oil dish, as described in No. 1 to No. 16.

For lunch, all types of fresh vegetables can be used. OLEOLOX should only be added AFTER the vegetables have been boiled. Season well!

---

* Editor's Note: LINOMELᴛᴍ International Patent Rights for Name & Production held by author.

** avoid chemically treated bananas

For the Unhealthy: Prepare mashed potatoes with OLE-OLOX and a little milk. Serve cooked, unpeeled potatoes as early as possible. Buckwheat is highly recommended as a substitute for potatoes.

Evening Meal (for the Unwell)

The evening meal should be very light and should be eaten early, around 6 pm. As an option, one can prepare a warm dish with rice, buckwheat, rolled oats, soya flakes, yeast flakes and other flakes available at health food stores. Depending on one's taste preferences, these dishes may be prepared as a soup or a stew and may be flavored with hearty sauces, added to vegetable stock and served as a tasty soup, or combined with sweet fruits. Fruits should preferably be eaten raw, possibly grated. For tasty addition, health food stores offer good, pre-made, yet healthy soya spreads.

GUIDELINES FOR NUTRITION
for the first 4 weeks of the "OIL-PROTEIN DIET"

The vital aspect of the Oil-Protein Diet consists of eliminating those fats which are difficult to digest. In their place, the easily digested and metabolized, "good fats" make up a primary component of the nutrition, enhancing energy and vitality.

Furthermore, the nutriments are put together in a way that preservatives, which act as respiratory toxins, are carefully eliminated. In contrast to preservatives, fresh and uncooked foods are rich in elements that support the independent absorption of oxygen by the organism. The framework of this model for nutrition deals with wholesome, total nutrition _ a regenerating diet. It is not to be confused with a "diet" that is simply non-stressful to the system. Many kinds of fresh vegetables are used raw and only fresh vegetables are steamed! Canned or preserved vegetables are avoided. Raw foods should be included in every meal, either in a raw salad plate or prepared in combination with warm meals. Fats are widely used, but are always in balance and harmonize with protein (eg. Quark with Flax Seed Oil, prepared in many variations, constitutes a considerable portion of this energy-rich and invigorating diet).

The Transition

On the transition day, only Linomel (250g) and nothing else should be consumed. With this, drink fresh juices, freshly squeezed fruit juices or pure, natural juices (without added sugar); also freshly pressed vegetable juices, (ie: carrot juice, celery with apple juice or red beet with apple juice are recommended). It is important to ensure that a warm drink be served at least three times a day_ herb teas, such as peppermint, rosehip or mallow tea. Sweeten only with honey. Do not add sugar in any form. Grape juice is permitted, and can be used to sweeten other unsweetened, pure juices. On occasion, black tea is allowed in the forenoon. For the very unwell, a "champagne-breakfast" consisting of champagne and Linomel is very acceptable. This "change-over day" is urgently recommended and is well tolerated, even by severely ill people.

Daily Plan:

Before breakfast: a glass of Sauerkraut Juice or Buttermilk.

Breakfast

A "Muesli" should be eaten regularly, prepared as follows:

Put 2 tablespoons of LINOMEL in a glass bowl. Cover this with a layer of fresh fruit in season, (ie: berries, cherries, apricots, peaches, grated apples). Now prepare a mixture made with Quark and Flax Seed Oil.

Add 3 tablespoons Flax Seed Oil to 100 - 125 g Quark, a little milk (2 Tblsp) and mix thoroughly until the oil has been totally absorbed. Lastly, add 1 tablespoon honey. In order to give it a new flavor every day, rosehip pulp, buckthorn juice, other fruit juices or ground nuts may be added. Butter is not recommended. Only herb teas should be served, but a cup of black tea is permitted on occasion.

At 10 a.m. drink a glass of freshly-pressed carrot juice, celery and apple juice, or beet and apple juice.

Lunch

a) Raw salad plate as an appetizer

Prepare a Quark/Flax Seed Oil mixture mayonnaise as follows:

Blend 2 tablespoons Flax Seed Oil and 2 tablespoons of milk with 2 tablespoons of Quark. Then add 2 tablespoons of lemon juice or apple cider vinegar and flavor with 1 teaspoon mustard and herbs _ (ie: marjoram, dill, parsley, etc). You may wish to add 2-3 Edengherkins or pickled cucumbers. As salt, Yehi herb salt is excellent. The Quark/Flax Seed Oil mixture, combined with mustard and a little banana is an excellent salad dressing. In the framework of the Oil-Protein Diet, the Quark/Flax Seed Oil mixture enhances the nutritional value of the raw foods; through the use of a variety of seasoning herbs, it is always possible to prepare new surprises, making the raw foods more interesting and appealing. For oil, use only Flax Seed oil. In addition to green lettuces, grated tubers such as carrots, kohlrabi, radishes, sauerkraut, comfrey root, cauli-flower, finely pureed or grated horse-radish and parsley are worth considering.

b) Cooked meals and steamed vegetables

Cooked meals and steamed vegetables may also consist of potatoes and above all, rice, buckwheat or millet. When adding fat, only OLEOLOX should be used (It tastes better on vegetables than Flax Seed Oil does). Vegetables are simply steamed or boiled in a little water, and before serving are mixed with a little OLEOLOX and seasoned with herbs. A good quality soya sauce can be used as a tasty supplement.

The Quark/Flax Seed Oil preparation can also be served with potato dishes and is especially tasty when flavored with caraway, chives, parsley or other herbs. When combining the Quark/Flax Seed Oil dish with potatoes, a little more Flax Seed Oil can be worked into the mixture (also see Chutneys No. 29 - 56).

c) Dessert

Serve the Quark/Flax Seed Oil dish similar to the one served for breakfast, substituting different fruits for variety. For a sweet Quark/Flax Seed Oil dish, combinations such as lemon-cream, wine-cream, banana-cream or vanilla-cream are delicious. Combining the dish with fresh fruit is always appropriate.

Around 4 p.m.

A small glass of natural wine, champagne or pure juice always combined with 1-2 tablespoons Linomel is recommended for the unwell. .

The evening

The evening meal should be light and should be served early, around 6 p.m. A warm meal may be prepared using rice, buckwheat, oat flakes, soya flakes or other flakes available at health food stores. Most easily tolerated and nourishing are the dishes made with buckwheat groats. These dishes can be prepared as a soup or in a more solid form and may be combined with a tasty sauce according to preference. Fat in the form of OLEOLOX should be liberally added also to sweet sauces and soups, making them nourishing and a richer source of energy.

To sweeten use only honey. Avoid sugars. I do not recommend wheat germ preparations; however, wheat germ oil (1 teaspoon, twice a day) can be added to the recovery program.

Strictly forbidden

For these first four weeks all animal fats, margarine and "salad oils" as well as butter are forbidden. Also all prepared meat products_ as they usually contain harmful preservatives. Canned meats are strictly prohibited and sausage meats should be completely avoided. Buy only pure, unsweetened fruit juices; the preparation of juice is very important and juices that contain preservatives are less valuable than those which have been left completely natural.

Also forbidden

Products from the "Konditorei" (pastry shop); especially the small pastries, which frequently contain harmful and biologically worthless fats are not encouraged.

Highly recommended

Drinking sauerkraut juice in the morning on an empty stomach and eating raw carrots, radishes, peppers, raw asparagus, raw cauliflower, kohlrabi and other preferably organic vegetables (that can be eaten raw) is highly recommended as a salad. Nuts, especially walnuts and brazil nuts should not be limited just to snack-time, but incorporated as an essential part of the nutrition plan. (See nut sauces with vegetables and/or salads No. 137-139). Nuts should also be used liberally in desserts.

Instead of candies or suckers, nuts (with dates, figs, or raisins) should be given to children. Within the framework of this approach to nutrition, seasoning liberally with fresh or dried herbs in winter is allowed and encouraged. Those who enjoy Flax Seed Oil need not be afraid of herbs and spices.

THE LINOMEL-MUESLI FOR BREAKFAST

Ingredients:

1 tsp honey
100 g Quark
3 tblsp milk
2 tblsp Linomel
3 tblsp Flax Seed Oil
Fresh fruits and fruit juices
Nuts

Preparation:

Putting 2 Tblsp Linomel in a small bowl, cover a layer of fruit in season. Choose mixed fruits (ie: fruit salad) or one type of fruit or berry on its own. In winter a coarsely-grated apple can be used in a number of ways, varied by adding cherry, blueberry or quince juice, or raisins, apricots, etc., soaked in apple juice.

QUARK/FLAX SEED OIL CREAM

Mix honey, milk and Flax Seed Oil, possibly in a blender. Add Quark gradually (in small portions) and stir until cream is smooth and the oil has been absorbed. A little milk can be added.

This mixture can be flavored differently every day by adding nuts, banana, lemon juice, orange-lemon juice mixed in a ratio of 2:1, cocoa, shredded coconut, rosehip pulp, fruit juices (always added last), vanilla, cinnamon, pineapple, etc. The layer of fruit is covered with the Quark/Flax Seed Oil Cream and then garnished with nuts or fruits.

Flax Oil makes the body absorb and use oxygen. Fresh air is important for the unwell. Strength permitting, exercise in fresh air is strongly recommended. Rest for balance and recovery is likewise important for the ailing. The bedridden patient often lacks the proper rhythm between resting and exerting available energies. Both are beneficial for recovery.

QUARK/FLAX SEED OIL

The Quark/Flax Seed Oil combination represents a modern-day phenomenon. This simple formula has prompted new scientific discoveries on how we can prevent and reverse many detriments to health which are caused by artificial fats, poor nutrition or other toxins. "Quark with Flax Seed Oil" gives many unhealthy people new strength, new life-impetus, vitality, and the will and power to regain health. It was the desire of the creator of this new scientific direction, the author of this book, to offer this help in a variety of ways, for as many patients as possible. I had discovered a new way of nutrition through the power in natural seed oils.

It is extremely important today that we use only fats and proteins of the highest quality. Today's modern theory that one should eat "low-fat foods" is incomplete, as these studies were based on inferior and nutritionally worthless fats.

Today the unwell need "good fats" which are easy to digest and metabolize, and which turn fat together with oxygen into energy. Combined with quark, these fats are water-soluble and easier to assimilate.

According to individual preference, the patient may prefer the sweeter breakfast Muesli or dessert fruit combinations, or lean towards the heartier flavors, enjoying oil with quark (ie: mayonnaise with salads) or combined with caraway, herbs and spices, on bread or with potatoes. In caring for an unwell person, these preferences should be discovered with skill and empathy. Variety is very important, since the

(continued)

patient should ingest an abundance of quark with Flax Seed Oil everyday. Fruits in season provide some variety, but should be served in various forms. For suggestions refer to the section on "Desserts". A love for the patient will help to generate new ideas. Love and caring for the ailing, is also a very important ingredient to the recipes listed here. Those who develop a love for this kind of nutrition while caring for the unhealthy, and also by making changes in their own life style, will be even better equipped to cook well for the patient and to provide tastier and more innovative dishes.

The Quark/Flax Seed Oil preparations represent a substantial part of the "OIL-PROTEIN DIET". The following recipes contain over 500 possible variations. Tailored according to individual taste, every patient should be able to enjoy these crucial regenerating foods. The Quark/Flax Seed Oil recipes form the core of "OIL-PROTEIN DIET."

1

QUARK/FLAX SEED OIL

QUARK/FLAX SEED OIL IN THE BREAKFAST-MUESLI:
(SEVERAL VARIATIONS)

●

Basic Ingredients:

2 tblsp Linomel
3 tblsp Flax Seed Oil
2 tblsp milk
100 g Quark
1 tsp honey
various added flavorings

■

Preparation:

Place 2 tablespoons Linomel in a small bowl and cover with a layer of diced raw seasonal fruit. Then prepare the Quark/Flax Seed Oil Cream as follows:
Combine Flax Seed Oil, milk and honey in a blender, gradually adding the Quark. When the mixture is smooth, flavor by adding vanilla, cinnamon, or combinations such as banana with lemon, orange juice, berries, etc.

2

QUARK/FLAX SEED OIL

Quark/Flax Seed Oil as Breakfast-Muesli with Blackberries and Vanilla

•

Ingredients:

Use basic recipe No. 1
3 tblsp blackberries
1/2 tsp vanilla

■

Preparation:

Top a small bowl of Linomel with a layer of
blackberries. Prepare a Vanilla Quark/Flax Seed
Oil Cream, sweetened by adding 1/2 teaspoon
vanilla and a little more honey than in the basic
recipe No.1. Pure blackberry juice poured over
this combination is delicious.

3

QUARK/FLAX SEED OIL

QUARK/FLAX SEED OIL AS BREAKFAST-MUESLI WITH BLACKBERRIES

•

Ingredients:

See basic recipe No. 1
1 cup blackberries
1 cup grape juice
or fresh grapes
1 tblsp walnuts

■

Preparation:

Cover the Linomel with half the ripe
blackberries, pour some grape juice over this.
Blend the other half of the blackberries with the
Quark/Flax Seed Oil Cream, then adding
walnuts. Blackberries require a little more
sweetening, achieved by adding grape juice and a
little honey.

4

QUARK/FLAX SEED OIL

QUARK/FLAX SEED OIL AS BREAKFAST-MUESLI WITH RASPBERRIES

•

Ingredients:

See basic recipe No. 1
1 cup raspberries

■

Preparation:

Put half the raspberries over the Linomel. Puree the other half with the Quark/Flax Seed Oil Cream; pour it over fruit.

---

5 ### QUARK/FLAX SEED OIL AS BREAKFAST-MUESLI WITH GOOSEBERRIES AND NUTS

•

Ingredients:

See basic recipe No. 1
2 tblsp gooseberries
3 tblsp red currants
3 tblsp pine nuts

■

Preparation:

Cover 2 tablespoons of Linomel with gooseberries. Blend red currants with the Quark/Flax Seed Oil Cream, pour this over the gooseberries; sprinkle with pine nuts.

6

QUARK/FLAX SEED OIL

QUARK/FLAX SEED OIL AS BREAKFAST-MUESLI WITH RED CURRANTS

●

Ingredients:

See basic recipe No. 1
1/2 lb. red currants

■

Preparation:

Divide the red currants into two equal portions.
Put half the currants over the Linomel. Blend the
other half into the Quark/Flax Seed Oil Cream
with honey and pour this mixture over the fruit
in the bowl. You can garnish this dish with a few
red or black currants, or a little of the white
Quark/Flax Seed Oil Cream.

7

QUARK/FLAX SEED OIL

QUARK/FLAX SEED OIL AS BREAKFAST-MUESLI WITH BLACK CURRANTS

•

Ingredients:

See basic recipe No. 1
2-3 heaping tblsp black currants
1/2 tsp vanilla

■

Preparation:

Cover 2 tablespoons of Linomel with black currants. Cover this with a Quark/Flax Seed Oil/Vanilla Cream as described in Recipe No. 1.

---

8 QUARK/FLAX SEED OIL AS BREAKFAST-MUESLI WITH GOOSEBERRIES AND VANILLA

•

Ingredients:

Basic ingredients as for Recipe No. 1
2 tblsp gooseberries
1/2 tsp vanilla

■

Preparation:

Cover 2 tablespoons Linomel with the well ripened, halved gooseberries. Then prepare the Quark/Flax Seed Oil/Vanilla Cream as in recipe No. 1, pour over the gooseberries and serve.

9

QUARK/FLAX SEED OIL

Quark/Flax Seed Oil as Breakfast-Muesli with Vanilla and Strawberries

•

Ingredients:

*Basic ingredients as for
Recipe No. 1
2 tblsp strawberries
1/2 tsp vanilla*

■

Preparation:

Cover 2 tablespoons of Linomel with strawberries. Then prepare the Quark/Flax Seed Oil Cream, adding 1/2 teaspoon of pure vanilla powder. Pour this cream over the strawberries and serve.

10

QUARK/FLAX SEED OIL

QUARK/FLAX SEED OIL AS BREAKFAST-MUESLI WITH BLUEBERRIES AND WALNUTS

•

Ingredients:

*Basic ingredients as for Recipe
No. 1
1 apple
(or any other fruit of choice)
1 tblsp blueberries
1 tblsp walnuts*

■

Preparation:

In a bowl, cover 2 tablespoons of Linomel with a grated apple or other fruit of choice. Blend 2-3 tablespoons of blueberries with the basic Quark/Flax Seed Oil Cream. Finally, add a handful of walnuts and mix VERY BRIEFLY. The walnuts should only be slightly crushed. This Quark/Flax Seed Oil Cream is very delicious.

11

QUARK/FLAX SEED OIL

QUARK/FLAX SEED OIL BREAKFAST-MUESLI WITH PURE, UNSWEETENED JUICES

•

Ingredients:

Basic ingredients as for
Recipe No. 1
1 apple
100 cc unsweetened juice
(cherry, blueberry or
red currant)

■

Preparation:

Cover 2 tablespoons Linomel with a grated apple. Pour 100 cc pure cherry or blueberry juice over this. Prepare the Quark/Flax Seed Oil Cream by first mixing the oil, milk and honey, and then gradually adding the Quark until the mixture is absolutely smooth. Lastly, add 1/2 teaspoon pure vanilla powder. Pour this over the fruit and serve without stirring.

12

QUARK/FLAX SEED OIL

QUARK/FLAX SEED OIL AS BREAKFAST-MUESLI WITH SEA-BUCKTHORN

•

Ingredients:

*Basic ingredients as for
Recipe No. 1
1 apple
The Juice of 1 orange
1 tblsp sea-buckthorn juice*

■

Preparation:

Cover 2 tablespoons Linomel with a grated apple and pour the orange juice over this. Prepare the Quark/Flax Seed Oil Cream as follows: Blend the Flax Seed Oil, milk, honey and Quark. Flavor with 1 tablespoon natural, unsweetened sea-buckthorn juice.
Cover the grated apple with the cream and serve.

13

QUARK/FLAX SEED OIL

QUARK/FLAX SEED OIL AS BREAKFAST-MUESLI WITH PEACHES (A)

●

Ingredients:

2 tblsp Linomel
3 tblsp Flax Seed Oil
2 tblsp milk
100 g Quark
1 tsp honey
2-3 ripened peaches

■

Preparation:

Put 2 tablespoons Linomel in a bowl and cover with 1 diced peach. Mix the Flax Seed, milk, honey and Quark as usual (see recipe No.1). Add a whole peach (without the stone), and blend it with the Quark/Flax Seed Oil Cream. Now cut up the third peach and fold it carefully into the mixture. Pour this mixture over the fruit in the bowl and perhaps garnish with a "cap" cut from one of the peaches. This Quark/Flax Seed Oil mixture is very delicious and season permitting, is recommended at the beginning of the Oil-Protein Diet.

14

QUARK/FLAX SEED OIL

QUARK/FLAX SEED OIL AS BREAKFAST-MUESLI WITH PEACHES (B)

•

Ingredients:

Basic recipe as for No. 1
2-4 nice peaches
Juice of (1) lemon

■

Preparation:

Cut 2 ripe peaches into small pieces and layer over the Linomel.
Mix the 2 other peaches into the Quark/Flax Seed Oil Cream and pour this over the fruit. Garnish with a nice piece of peach. If there are only enough peaches for the fruit layer, then the juice of a lemon can be used to flavor the Quark/Flax Seed Oil Cream.

15

QUARK/FLAX SEED OIL

QUARK/FLAX SEED OIL AS BREAKFAST-MUESLI WITH PINEAPPLE AND GINGER

•

Ingredients:

Basic recipe as for No. 1
2 slices pineapple
Pinch of cinnamon
Pinch of ginger
Pinch of salt

■

Preparation:

Put 2 tablespoons Linomel in a bowl. Drain small pieces of fresh pineapple which have been soaked in diluted salt water for 1/2 hour and layer them over the Linomel. Prepare the Quark/Flax Seed Oil Cream as described for Basic Recipe No. 1, adding a pinch of cinnamon and of freshly grated ginger. Pour this cream over the pineapple. Do not combine this mixture long prior to serving because the pineapple will develop a bitter taste if it is left in the Flax Seed Oil. Pineapple must NOT be blended into the Quark/Flax Seed Oil Cream.

16

QUARK/FLAX SEED OIL

QUARK/FLAX SEED OIL MAYONNAISE
(BASIC RECIPE)

●

Ingredients:

3 tblsp Flax Seed Oil
3 tblsp milk
3 tblsp Quark
1 tblsp lemon juice
and/or
2 tblsp apple cider vinegar
1 tblsp mustard
1/2 tsp Yehi-Herb salt

■

Preparation:

In a blender, combine oil and milk with Quark.
Add mustard, lemon juice, vinegar and salt. This
Quark/Flax Seed Oil Mayonnaise lends itself to
many wonderful variations.

17-24

QUARK/FLAX SEED OIL

QUARK/FLAX SEED OIL MAYONNAISE,
(MORE VARIATIONS)

●

Use the Basic Recipe and amounts as in No.16, adding:

17. *1 tblsp marjoram, blend well.*
18. *1/2 tblsp marjoram and 1/2 tsp dill.*
19. *1 tblsp dill, finely chopped, or powder.*
20. *Soya Sauce No.63, described with Chicory Salad;*
     Add 3 tablespoons of this sauce to the mayonnaise.
21. *Puree 5-6 dill pickles with the mayonnaise.*
     The herb vinegar of the pickles can also be used
     (preservative-free).
22. *Add 1 tblsp finely chopped chives AFTER blending*
     the mayonnaise.
23. *Puree 100-200 g parsley with the mayonnaise.*
24. *The basic recipe or the variations No.17-23 are*
     further modified by adding 1 tablespoon pumpkin
     seed oil.

■

All the mayonnaises are recommended as salad
dressings, dips and sauces for raw salad platters. They
can be further varied by combining with the recipes
described for salads (see No. 57-77); with sauces
(see No. 104, 106-107, 137-139, 144-145).

25

QUARK/FLAX SEED OIL

QUARK/FLAX SEED OIL AS A SPREAD ON BREAD (CARAWAY-QUARK)

•

Ingredients:

125 g Quark
2 tblsp milk
3 tblsp Flax Seed Oil
Pinch of salt
1 tsp ground caraway seed
1 tblsp whole caraway seed

Other possible combinations with:
1 tsp red paprika
1 tblsp onion, finely chopped

■

Preparation:

Blend the Quark, Flax Seed Oil, milk and salt to a firm paste. Add the ground and the whole caraway seed, mix well and put this mixture into a small bowl. The red paprika and the finely chopped onion can be served separately or mixed into the spread. Serve as a bread spread or with potato dishes.

QUARK/FLAX SEED OIL

QUARK/FLAX SEED OIL AS A SPREAD WITH HERB-CHEESE

●

Ingredients:

125 g Quark
2 tblsp milk
3 tblsp Flax Seed Oil
2 tblsp grated herb cheese

■

Preparation:

Blend the Quark, Flax Seed Oil and milk into
a thick paste, put into a small bowl.
Add 2 tablespoons grated herb cheese and let the
mixture stand for 1/2 hour. This is delicious with
potatoes or as a spread. The goat-cheese Geska is
highly suitable.

27

QUARK/FLAX SEED OIL

QUARK/FLAX SEED OIL AS A SPREAD WITH SPICY HERBS

●

Ingredients:

125 g Quark
2 tblsp milk
3 tblsp Flax Seed Oil
Pinch of herb salt (aromatic salt)
1/2 tsp dill
1 tblsp marjoram
2 garlic cloves

■

Preparation:

Mix the Quark, Flax Seed Oil and milk to form a thick paste and put this in a small bowl. Add 2 crushed garlic cloves, the dill and marjoram. Let the mixture stand 1/2 hour. Very tasty with potatoes, but especially good as a spread.

28

QUARK/FLAX SEED OIL

QUARK/FLAX SEED OIL AS A SPREAD
(SPICY, WITH GARLIC)

●

Ingredients:

5 tblsp Flax Seed Oil
2 tblsp condensed milk
125 g Quark
1 large garlic clove
1 tsp whole caraway
1/2 tsp ground caraway
1/2 tsp aromatic salt
Pinch of thyme

■

Preparation:

Combine the Quark, milk and Flax Seed Oil in
a blender. Add the aromatic salt, a pinch of
thyme and the ground and whole caraway seed
to the Quark/Flax Seed Oil mixture. Put this
into a small bowl and add a large (or 2 small)
clove of pressed garlic. Stir into the mixture and
set aside to allow the flavor to penetrate. This
spicy preparation can be used on bread
or with potatoes.
A further variation is to simply mix a heaping
teaspoon of fresh, finely chopped or dried
marjoram into this dressing.

QUARK/FLAX SEED OIL AS A CHUTNEY SIDE DISH

Chutneys are very tasty and aromatically spiced side dishes, eaten in India and the Orient as a side dish with rice.

The Quark/Flax Seed Oil preparations described here in the form of different chutneys, easily enhance both the appeal and nutritional value of menus served with vegetables and potatoes, rice, buckwheat or millet dishes. The following recipes are tasty, easily varied and expanded.

QUARK/FLAX SEED OIL

Quark/Flax Seed Oil as Chutney
basic mixture (A) & (B)

•

Ingredients:

BASIC MIXTURE (A)

3 tblsp Flax Seed Oil
2 tblsp milk
125 g Quark
Aromatic salt

BASIC MIXTURE (B)

1 large, tart apple
2 tblsp pure cherry juice
or
2 tblsp red beet juice

■

Preparation:

(A) Flax Seed Oil, milk, Quark and salt are blended into a fairly firm paste. This Paste (A) is put in a small bowl.

(B) About 1/3 or 1/4 of this paste is left in the blender. While still blending, add the chopped apple. Puree with the Quark/Flax seed Oil paste while adding cherry juice or red beet juice. Pour into a second dish.

31

QUARK/FLAX SEED OIL

Quark/Flax Seed Oil as Chutney, (Variation I)

•

Ingredients:

BASIC MIXTURE (No. 29/A)
1 tbs ground caraway seed
1 tbs whole caraway seed

■

Preparation:

The Basic Chutney Mixture No.29/A (Quark, Flax Seed Oil, milk, salt) is briefly pureed with the ground and the whole caraway seed and is served as a side dish with potatoes or vegetables.

32

Quark/Flax Seed Oil as Chutney (Variation II)

•

Ingredients:

BASIC MIXTURE (No. 29/A)
200 g parsley

■

Preparation:

The BASIC MIXTURE is pureed with all the parsley and served as a side dish to potatoes; the vegetable platter or a salad platter.

QUARK/FLAX SEED OIL

Quark/Flax Seed Oil as Chutney
(Variation III)

●

Ingredients:

BASIC MIXTURE
(No. 29/A)

1 tblsp onion,
finely chopped
1 tsp paprika
1 tsp caraway
2 dill pickles

■

Preparation:

Pour the Basic Mixture No. 29/A into a bowl,
adding caraway, paprika and onion. Adding the
dill pickles, cut lengthwise or sliced. Ideal for
complementary potatoes, vegetable platters, etc.

QUARK/FLAX SEED OIL

QUARK/FLAX SEED OIL AS CHUTNEY
(VARIATION IV)

●

Ingredients:

BASIC MIXTURE
(No.29/A)

1 pickled herring
Pickled onions

■

Preparation:

Remove the scales from the sour herring, cut into
small pieces and mix with plenty of pickled
onions into the BASIC MIXTURE
Relished by enthusiasts!

35

QUARK/FLAX SEED OIL

QUARK/FLAX SEED OIL AS CHUTNEY
(VARIATION V)

●

Ingredients:

BASIC MIXTURE
(No.29/A)

1/2 apple
1 piece horseradish
1 cm thick,
(adjust to taste)

■

Preparation:

Blend the horseradish while adding the milk.
Then add Flax Seed Oil and Quark (see BASIC
MIXTURE). Lastly, add half an apple and puree.
Excellent with a wide variety of dishes. This
chutney offers great health benefits for the liver.

36

QUARK/FLAX SEED OIL

QUARK/FLAXSEED OIL AS CHUTNEY
(VARIATION VI)

●

Ingredients:

Basic Mixture I (No.29)
Basic Mixture II (No.30)

Ingredients for
Variations 1-5
are optional

■

Preparation:

With the Basic Mixture I and variations No.1-5,
other flavors may be developed by simply using
the Basic Mixture II simultaneously. Many
variations may thus be achieved. Take note also
of the color effects of Basic Mixture No.30.

37

QUARK/FLAX SEED OIL

QUARK/FLAX SEED OIL AS CHUTNEY A LA TSCHA-TSCHI (TSCHA - TSCHI BASIC MIXTURE I)

●

Ingredients:

3 tblsp Flax Seed Oil
2 tblsp milk
100 g Quark
50 g walnuts
Juice of 1/2 lemon
2 garlic cloves
1/2 tsp aromatic salt

■

Preparation:

Blend the Flax Seed Oil, milk, Quark, and lemon juice. Lastly, add a handful of walnuts, blend and pour into a bowl. Stir 2 pressed garlic cloves into the Quark/Flax Seed Oil mixture.

38

QUARK/FLAX SEED OIL

TSCHA-TSCHI BASIC MIXTURE II

●

Ingredients:

*3 tblsp of the
Tscha-Tschi Basic
Mixture I
1 apple
1/2 cup pure cherry
juice
or red beet juice
mixed with a little
apple juice*

■

Preparation:

Puree the Tscha-Tschi Basic Mixture I with the
apple and cherry juice, or the red beet
with apple juice.
This Tscha-Tschi Basic Mixture II can be varied
by combining with Basic Mixture Tscha-Tschi I
and by adding spices and herbs.

39

QUARK/FLAX SEED OIL

Tscha-Tschi
(variation 1)
●

Ingredients:

Tscha-Tschi Basic Mixture I
1 fresh green cucumber

■

Preparation:

Using the Basic Mixture of Quark/Flax Seed Oil, milk, lemon, walnuts and garlic is prepared as previously described above. The cucumber is cut into small cubes and mixed with the Tscha-Tschi Mixture. Variations: Add 1-2 teaspoon of the red Basic Tscha-Tschi II. Suitable to complement a vegetable platter, potatoes, or a raw salad platter.

40

Tscha-Tschi
(variation 2)
●

Ingredients:

I tblsp Tscha-Tschi I
1 tblsp Apple Tscha-Tschi II
2 tblsp sweet & sour paprikas, cut into small cubes

■

Preparation:

Mix equal amounts of the red and white Tscha-Tschi, and stir in the finely cubed sweet & sour paprikas.

41

QUARK/FLAX SEED OIL

TSCHA-TSCHI
(VARIATION 3)

●

Ingredients:

1 tblsp white Tscha-Tschi I
1 tblsp red Tscha-Tschi
A pinch of powdered coriander

■

■

Preparation:

Mix everything well and let stand to allow for the flavor to penetrate.

42

TSCHA-TSCHI
(VARIATION 4)

●

Ingredients:

1 tblsp white Tscha-Tschi
1 tblsp red Tscha-Tschi
1 tsp tomato catsup

■

Preparation:

Mix everything. Excellent as a side dish.

43

QUARK/FLAX SEED OIL

TSCHA-TSCHI
(VARIATION 5)

•

Ingredients:

1 tblsp white Tscha-Tschi
1 tblsp red Tscha-Tschi
1 tblsp pritamin

■

Preparation:

Mix both Tscha-Tschi Basic Mixtures together
with pritamin, and serve as a side dish
with vegetables, salad platters, potatoes or rice.

QUARK/FLAX SEED OIL

TSCHA-TSCHI
(VARIATION 6)

●

Ingredients:

2 tblsp white Tscha-Tschi
2 tblsp red Tscha-Tschi
1/2 tsp cayenne pepper
1 tsp paprika
1 tsp mustard

■

Preparation:

Mix both Tscha-Tschi Basic Mixtures
with the seasonings.
Very suitable as a side dish in this form.
Further Variations:
Combined with pickled pearl onions, mixed
pickles, sweet & sour paprikas, pieces of apple or
fresh and finely cubed cucumber.
Eat as a side-dish with vegetables or as described
under Chutneys.

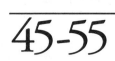

45-55

QUARK/FLAX SEED OIL

DIFFERENT TSCHA-TSCHI VARIATIONS

•

*To 3-4 tablespoons of the Tscha-Tschi Basic Mixture I,
Tscha-Tschi II, or a combination of both, add the following
ingredients:*

45.   *1 tsp shredded coconut or*

46.   *1 tsp cranberries or*

47.   *1 tsp candied orange peel or*

48.   *1 steamed apple with grated almonds,etc.*

49-50 *The combinations of Tscha-Tschi Mixture I or II,
        and II mixed with Soya Sauces No.144 a-d are
        very good.*

*All of the Chutneys, including the Tscha-Tschi recipes can
easily be varied:*

51.   *by adding 1 tblsp pumpkin seed oil*

52.   *by adding 1 tblsp pumpkin seed oil and 1/2 tsp honey*

53.   *by adding 3-5 dashes Tabasco seasoning*

54.   *by adding 1 tblsp pumpkin seed oil, 1/2 tsp honey,
        and 5 dashes Tabasco; excellent with nut and garlic
        Tscha-Tschi recipes No.37-44.*

55.   *Adding a pinch of ginger or coriander give these
        Chutney recipes an interesting note; especially in
        combination with pumpkin seed oil and a little
        honey.*

56

QUARK/FLAX SEED OIL

QUARK/FLAX SEED OIL MIXTURE
(AVOIDING UNFAVORABLE COMBINATIONS)

●

*Be careful with
ingredients:*

*grapefruit,
pineapple,
fresh pureed tomatoes*

■

Preparation:

Quark/Flax Seed Oil mixtures with grapefruit
tend to bitter. The same is true for pineapple
when it is mixed into the Quark/Flax Seed Oil
mixture. While pureed tomatoes do *not* mix well
with the Quark/Flax Seed Oil mixture, tomato
catsup can be used.

SALADS

The value of a diet incorporating raw foods is being increasingly acknowledged everywhere. "We eat a lot of salad" is the answer that is frequently heard today when someone wants to document that they are following modern progressive nutrition. They are referring almost exclusively to the greenhouse/hot house head lettuce, garnished with a few tomatoes at best.

The use of almost every kind of vegetable, in particular tubers such as radishes, root celery, red beets, leeks, cauliflower, fennel, cabbage or red cabbage, is only interesting if one understands how to prepare them so that they are not hard and bulky - but soft. This is achieved in the recipes presented in this book by using an abundance of oil in combination with some Quark and many cooking herbs and spices. The flavor of the salad platters that are prepared in this manner is easily varied; the Quark/Flax Seed Oil mayonnaise can be prepared in many different ways on the same salad platter - with chives, dill, caraway or mustard in combination with banana on the one hand, or using the aforementioned variations of the soya salad sauces on the other hand. Once one has mastered the suggestions outlined here, it becomes a daily joy to surprise the family with new and interesting salad sauces. "Oh, these delicious sauces!" I hear so often from those who were once opposed to the hard and bland salads.

(continued)

When the homemaker places one or two extra dishes of delicious mayonnaise on the table, the salad platter pays tribute to their imagination and inventiveness.

The variety of the salad platters is determined largely by the marketplace and the season. With every improvement that comes from using "recipes", it remains essential that the person preparing meals understands how to create new nuances in flavor when preparing the salad sauces. When the tender dandelion is available for the salad platter, dandelion salad should be on the daily menu. However it should be flavored differently every day, for example, by adding onions or garlic. Other possibilities for altering the same salad in a new form include flavoring with soya sauce, tomato paste, pritamin and pumpkin seed oil. Sweet & sour red paprikas or pearl onions can help achieve other tasty ways of presenting the same valuable dishes such as dandelion salad. This is only an illustration of how to, and in spite of all the recipes, loving preparation goes far beyond them.

SALADS

RED BEETS WITH HORSERADISH

●

Ingredients:

1 lb. red beets
1 tblsp caraway
1 tblsp grated horseradish
1/2 tsp aromatic salt
2 tblsp Flax Seed Oil
2 tblsp milk
1 tblsp Quark
1 apple
3 tblsp apple cider vinegar

■

Preparation:

Wash the beets thoroughly and cook them
unpeeled until tender (test with a fork).
Peel and slice the beets.
In a blender, first combine the Quark, Flax Seed
Oil and milk, then adding the grated horseradish
(if the horseradish is whole, it is better to blend it
first with some milk). Now add the vinegar, salt
and caraway to the mixture, finally adding
a diced apple.

57

(continued)

You can proceed by mixing the very thinly sliced beets with this Quark/Flax Seed Oil mixture and serve it after it has stood long enough for the flavor to penetrate.

Another tasty option: Slice the beets 5-7 mm thick and layer them in a dish. Intersperse the layers with plenty of the fairly firm Quark/Flax Seed Oil mixture. This dish should also be allowed to stand for at least one half hour before serving.

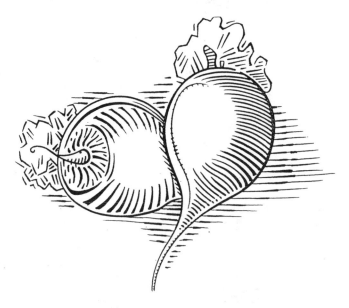

58

SALADS

Cucumber Salad, well seasoned

●

Ingredients:

1 long cucumber
1/2 tsp aromatic salt
3 tblsp Flax Seed Oil
3 tblsp milk
1 tblsp Quark
1 tblsp apple cider vinegar
2 garlic cloves
1 pepper

■

Preparation:

Wash the cucumber but do not peel it. Slice it finely with a cucumber knife, adding salt. Prepare the sauce with Quark, milk, Flax Seed Oil and apple cider vinegar. Mix in pressed garlic.

a) The cucumbers can be mixed with this mayonnaise and served.

b) Remove the seeds from the pepper, chop it very finely, and mix it into the cucumber salad as described in (a).

59

SALADS

TOMATO SALAD

●

Ingredients:

1 lb. tomatoes
3 nice peppers
2 large onions
1/2 tsp aromatic salt
1/2 tsp pepper
1 tsp paprika
1 tblsp dill or
parsley
optional: lemon juice

■

Preparation:

Wash the tomatoes and seed the peppers.
Thinly slice the tomatoes, peppers and onions,
and mix them with salt, pepper, paprika and dill.
Let stand for about 1/2 hour to let the flavor
penetrate. This salad can be served with or
without lemon juice, and with or without oil.
Both flavor variations are excellent.

60

SALADS

TOMATO SALAD
(EAST INDIAN STYLE I)

•

Ingredients:

1 lb tomatoes
salt
black pepper
white pepper
3 tblsp Flax Seed Oil
3 tblsp apple cider vinegar
1/2 tsp sweet paprika
1 cup shredded coconut
1 cup water

■

Preparation:

Slice the tomatoes and mix them with a
dressing marinade made from the oil, vinegar,
black and white pepper, and salt to taste. Put the
shredded coconut in the blender with a cup of
water and puree until fine (do not use rancid
products). Pour this coconut milk over the
tomatoes, letting it stand for at least 1/2 hour to
let the flavor penetrate, then serve.

SALADS

TOMATO SALAD
(EAST INDIAN STYLE II)

●

Ingredients:

1 lb. tomatoes
salt
black pepper
3 tblsp Flax Seed Oil
1 tblsp pumpkin seed oil
3 tblsp apple cider vinegar
3 tblsp celery leaves,
finely chopped

■

Preparation:

Mix thinly sliced tomatoes with a salad marinade
made from the oils and vinegar. Salt and pepper
to taste. Then add the finely chopped,
tender celery leaves.

62

SALADS

Tomato Salad
with Peppermint

•

Ingredients:

1 lb. tomatoes
2 large onions
Salt & pepper
2-3 peppermint leaves
1/2 tsp honey
A pinch of ginger
1/2 cup Flax Seed Oil
1 tblsp pumpkin seed oil

■

Preparation:

Slice the tomatoes. For the marinade, mix finely
chopped onions and chopped peppermint leaves
with the oil, vinegar, salt, pepper,
honey and ginger. Add the tomato slices, mix
well and serve.

63

SALADS

CHICORY SALAD WITH CRESS

•

Ingredients:

2 medium chicory
50 g cress
3 tblsp soya sauce
3 tblsp water
2 tblsp vinegar
2 garlic cloves
1 tsp honey
1 tsp shredded coconut
2 tblsp Flax Seed Oil
2 tblsp pumpkin seed oil

■

Preparation:

(A) Cut the chicory into 5 cm wide strips. Mix together the soya sauce, water, vinegar, garlic and honey. To half this mixture, add 1 teaspoon shredded coconut, 1 teaspoon Flax Seed Oil and 2 tablespoons pumpkin seed oil, and blend. Mix the chicory with this sauce, piling it in the center of a plate or salad platter.
(B) Into the second half of the sauce (without the coconut), blend 1 tablespoon Flax Seed Oil and mix this sauce with the cress. Arrange this mixture at the head of the chicory pile, making a delicate and decorative ring around the chicory. The contrasting flavors, chicory/soya sauce/cress are very appealing.

64

SALADS

GREEN BEANS AS SALAD

•

Ingredients:

1 lb. green beans
1 large onion
Some savory
1 tblsp soya sauce
2 tblsp Flax Seed Oil
1 tblsp milk or buttermilk
(own preference)
Some paprika
Black, white and cayenne pepper

■

Preparation:

Wash and de-string the beans and break them into pieces. Boil beans with a few leaves of savory (or powdered savory if necessary) in a little water or steam them until tender. *Do not overcook them.* In a bowl, prepare a marinade by mixing the Flax Seed Oil, milk, finely chopped onion, soya sauce and seasoning. After the beans have cooled, add them to this marinade and mix well.
This bean salad can also be prepared with the following:
Turkish Salad Sauce No. 145
Soya Salad Sauce, sweet, spicy No. 144
Syrian Side-dish(i) No. 137
Syrian Side-dish(ii) No. 138
Nut/Paprika Sauce No. 139

SALADS

ONION SALAD
WITH GREEN BEANS

●

Ingredients:

1/2 lb. onions
1/2 lb. green beans
1 cup Flax Seed Oil
1/2 cup apple cider vinegar
1/2 tsp honey
1/2 tsp paprika
aromatic salt

■

Preparation:

Cut the onions into large pieces, depending on size, into quarters or eighths. Boil them in water to which honey has been added. Boil only until they turn "glassy". Steam the beans separately or boil them in a little water. Both the drained onions and beans are added to a marinade made by mixing the Flax Seed Oil, vinegar, honey, salt, paprika; and possibly adding soya sauce and aromatic salt. Mix well. This is an excellent side dish with cooked vegetables, on a vegetable platter or a large salad platter.

SALADS

CARROTS FOR THE RAW SALAD PLATTER

●

Ingredients:

1/2 lb carrots
1 orange
A pinch of anise

■

Preparation:

Wash and finely grate, mixing them with the
juice of 1 orange. Add a little anise for another
flavor variation.

SALADS

CELERY SALAD

•

Ingredients:

*2 medium sized
celery roots
Salad Sauce No. 144,
or No. 145, or
Chutney No. 29 or
Banana-cream No. 1*

■

Preparation:

The celery tubers are best cleaned with a brush (the little rootlets can be removed). Boil until tender in water to which 1 tablespoon apple cider vinegar, wine vinegar or a little lemon juice has been added. After about 15 minutes they will peel easily. Cut the celery into small slices or pieces. When it has cooled, mix it with Salad Sauce No. 144, 145, 146 or with the Chutney Paste No. 29-30, which contains apple.

You can also make a clear celery salad by simply mixing the celery with 2 tablespoons apple cider vinegar, 2 tablespoons apple juice, 2 tablespoons Flax Seed Oil and some celery salt or aromatic salt. Combinations with Nut Sauce No. 145, with apple as in No. 146 or celery with the Banana lemon cream No. 1, are especially delicious.

SALADS

CUCUMBER SALAD

•

Ingredients:

2 long cucumbers
2 tblsp finely chopped
fresh dill
or
1 heaping teaspoon
dried dill
Quark/Flax Seed Oil
mayonnaise No. 16

■

Preparation:

Wash and thinly slice unpeeled cucumbers.
Sprinkle with a little aromatic salt and let stand
for 1/2 hour to draw the juice from them.
Prepare the Basic Quark/Flax Seed Oil
mayonnaise No. 16, possibly with dill pickles
adding plenty of fresh dill or dill powder. The
cucumber salad improves in flavor if left to stand
a while - especially when dried herbs are used.

SALADS

Carrot Salad, cooked

●

Ingredients:

1 lb carrots
1/2 cup Flax Seed Oil
1/2 cup apple cider vinegar
2 tblsp soya sauce
1/2 tsp ginger
salt
pepper

■

Preparation:

Wash the carrots and either boil them with a little water or briefly steam them, not letting them become too soft. Cut the carrots into 3 cm long sections. After they have cooled, combine them with a marinade made from oil, vinegar, salt, pepper, ginger and soya sauce.

Other variations:
The carrot salad can be prepared with any of the different Quark/Flax Seed Oil mayonnaise No. 16-24.

SALADS

SALAD PLATTER WITH MIXED SALADS

●

Ingredients:

3 tblsp Quark
3 tblsp Flax Seed Oil
3 tblsp milk
1 tblsp mustard
1/2 tsp honey or
1/2 banana
3 dill pickles
3 tblsp apple cider vinegar
Juice of 1/2 lemon
Various types of Green lettuce
Red beets
Raw celery
Parsley root
Kohlrabi
Green beans
etc.

■

(continued)

(continued)

Preparation:

One type of green lettuce, either leaf lettuce,
finely cut endive, corn salad or cress is always
used in preparing the raw vegetable salads.
Arrange the green lettuce in the center of the
salad platter. The other salads, such as finely
grated kohlrabi or red beet salad (raw or cooked),
are arranged in separate little piles.
Prepare mayonnaise in a blender, using the
Quark, Flax Seed Oil, milk, mustard, dill pickles
and a little salt. Divide this mayonnaise into
several small bowls. Mix the mayonnaise of one
bowl with either the finely grated cauliflower,
finely grated comfrey root, finely cut celery root
with 1/4 grated apple, red beets with ground
walnuts, cucumber slices with dill, or green beans
with finely chopped onions. Puree the rest of the
mayonnaise in a blender with 1/2 banana and
pour this over the greens in the center of the
platter. The various raw vegetable salads are now
arranged in little piles around the green salad. In
this way, the Quark/Flax Seed Oil preparation is
always given a different flavor, making the platter
more appealing and interesting to the patient.

SALADS

LEEK AS SALAD

●

Ingredients:

1 lb. leeks
Salad Sauce No. 144
or
Quark/Flax Seed Oil
mayonnaise No. 16

■

Preparation:

Wash the leeks carefully, cutting them into thin slices. Steam very briefly or boil until half done. Remove leeks from the water and prepare as a salad using salad sauces or the Quark/Flax Seed Oil mayonnaise as described for the salad platter in No. 70. The cooking water may be used as a vegetable broth (ie: for the evening buckwheat-groats soup).

SALADS

Raw Cabbage Salad

●

Ingredients:

1 small green cabbage
1/2 cup Flax Seed Oil
2 tblsp pumpkin seed oil
1 onion
2 garlic cloves
1 tblsp soy sauce
1 tblsp coconut flakes

■

Preparation:

Remove the cabbage core and grate the leaves.
Briefly heat the onions and the crushed garlic in
the Flax Seed Oil. Remove from heat, adding the
coconut flakes and soya sauce. Then add the
grated cabbage to the heated sauce. Add
pumpkin seed oil and mix.
This cabbage salad may be served hot or cold. To
give it a more delicate flavor, the completed salad
may be mixed with a little condensed milk.

73

SALADS

CABBAGE SALAD, EAST INDIAN STYLE

●

Ingredients:

1 lb. green cabbage
1 large onion
Black pepper
1 leek
A little ginger
1/2 cup Flax Seed Oil
3 tblsp apple cider vinegar
A pinch of salt

■

Preparation:

Finely slice the cabbage. Either blanch it very briefly in boiling water or use it raw. Prepare the marinade by mixing the oil, vinegar, salt, pepper, and a good pinch of ginger. The onion and the very tender yellow parts of the leek are sliced very fine and mixed in with the marinade. Now mix the cabbage with the marinade and let stand for about 1/2 hour before serving.

SALADS

Onion Salad as a Side Dish

●

Ingredients:

4 large onions
1 pepper or cayenne pepper
1 tart apple
1/2 lemon
2 tblsp Flax Seed Oil
Salt
A dash of black or white pepper

Optional:
1 tblsp milk

■

Preparation:

The onions are first thinly sliced, then finely chopped. The apple can be grated coarsely or very fine. Chop the pepper very fine. Mix together the lemon, Flax Seed Oil, salt and pepper. You can reduce the sharpness by adding 1 tablespoon milk. This also helps to bind the lemon juice and the oil. Now add the onions, apple and peppers to the sauce. This dish may be added to the salad platter or served with a Quark/Flax Seed Oil Mayonnaise. It is also suitable as a side dish to potatoes with vegetables, rice dishes with vegetables or tasty buckwheat dishes.

75

SALADS

HERB SALAD

●

Ingredients:

1 leek	*Parsley*
Borage	*1/2 cup Flax Seed Oil*
Spinach	*1 lemon*
Sorrel	*1 tsp honey*
Marjoram,	*2 garlic cloves*
(preferably fresh)	*150 g buckwheat groats*
Thyme	*or dried green spelt*
Lemon balm	*2 tblsp OLEOLOX*
Dill	*(see pg. vii)*

■

Preparation:

Only the pale and tender parts of the leek are finely
cut. Take a handful of all the other herbs and finely
chop them. Prepare a marinade made with the Flax
Seed Oil, lemon juice, honey and crushed garlic, and
mix with all the herbs. Let stand for 1 hour to allow the
flavors to penetrate. Lightly saute the spelt or
buckwheat in the OLEOLOX and add to th herb salad.
This herb salad is very tasty, appreciated by all
enthusiasts, and is extremely healthy and easily
digested. Above all, this fine salad can be used as a side
dish to rice dishes with vegetables or to potato dishes
with cooked vegetables.

76

SALADS

ASPARAGUS SALAD WITH MAYONNAISE

●

Ingredients:

2 lb. asparagus
250 g Quark
150g Flax Seed Oil
75 g milk
5 dill pickles
1 tblsp mustard
Salt
1/2 tsp honey

■

Preparation:

Prepare the asparagus as usual and tie it in bundles with thread or string. Bring the slightly salted water to a boil before adding the asparagus. Cook until tender.
Remove the bundles from the water, let them cool and cut into 5 cm long pieces.
Prepare the mayonnaise as follows:
Quark, Flax Seed Oil, milk and mustard are mixed well in a blender. To this, add 5 dill pickles and puree.
Flavor with 1/2 teaspoon honey, salt to taste, and/or a little soya sauce. Mix the asparagus pieces with the mayonnaise.
This asparagus salad is excellent in combination with raw, sweet, tender peas, or with cooked and cooled carrots, cut into strips.
It may be served as an appetizer or as part of the salad platter.

SALADS

DANDELION SALAD

●

Ingredients:

*250 g young, tender
dandelions,(the narrow
leaf variety is best)
1 onion
3 tblsp Flax Seed Oil
2 tblsp milk
2 tblsp Quark
Aromatic salt
2 dill pickles*

■

Preparation:

The tender, well-washed dandelions (including the
short root stocks) are cut very small. Chop the leaves
finely; the blossoms can also be used. Separately, prepare a mayonnaise using Flax Seed Oil, milk, Quark,
1 tablespoon apple cider vinegar, 2 dill pickles, some
aromatic salt, and possibly some mustard.
Finally, mix the finely chopped onions and the
mayonnaise (not in a blender). Then mix the
mayonnaise with the dandelions. The flavor of this
salad is enhanced if it is left to stand in a cool place
for 1 hour before serving.

BUCKWHEAT, RICE AND OTHER CEREALS, POTATOES, LEGUMES, ETC.

These side dishes to vegetables or salads are also very important. Potatoes are often too heavy for sick people or for the mentally active to digest. For example, if a student or an athlete attempts to adhere strictly to the diet recommended for the unwell, he/she would be surprised at how their performance levels improve. Potatoes burden the system more heavily than buckwheat. The Russians still use very much buckwheat in their main courses. In the Far East, rice is preferred; both are important. When using rice, whole unpolished rice should be chosen. Several recipes may be found in this chapter, including preparation of buckwheat (which is especially recommended for the unwell) but I ask you to pay attention to and to test the following: if the various vegetables are prepared with plenty of fats and are well spiced, the buckwheat or rice is more suitably prepared as a simple, neutral dish. The savory and strongly flavored vegetables are best complemented by the bland and neutral, buckwheat groats or rice. Nettle salad for example, prepared with many spices, garlic, paprika and pepper, is excellent in combination with buckwheat groats that have been cooked in plain water and served separately. In the Far East, the rice dish is almost always neutral. In contrast, the side dishes are savory and interesting. Our meat-centered meals, which we tend to refer to as being "full of variety", are really inflexible and deficient because of the emphasis placed on one-sided meat dishes, ignoring the possibilities that spices and herbs offer the whole cuisine. Once spices and herbs are rediscovered, we can again venture to serve neutral dishes such as buckwheat, rice or cracked wheat. It is a matter of seeing the whole picture, not simply its components.

(continued)

Buckwheat, which is so valuable for the unwell, can be simply boiled in water and served daily as a neutral side dish to vegetables (just as rice is served in the Far East). One even becomes accustomed to this dish without salt, if the vegetables are zestily prepared. Buckwheat can be served just as potato dumplings, always flavored mildly and quite neutral. In contrast, tasty and strongly spiced buckwheat variations (prepared according to the Russian model) or Far Eastern rice dishes (use only whole rice, please), offer new and interesting possibilities of natural and wholesome nutrition for the unwell and healthy alike.

78

BUCKWHEAT, RICE, POTATOES, LEGUMES, ETC.

BUCKWHEAT PORRIDGE
BASIC RECIPE

●

Ingredients:

1 cup buckwheat
3 cups water
(The whole buckwheat
kernel or fine buckwheat
groats may be used.)

■

Preparation:

Putting the buckwheat into cold water, simmer
for 1 hr over a very low flame
(electric plate No.2) to let it swell.
This basic preparation can be used in many ways:

added to vegetable broth, in soups together with
milk or buttermilk, as a filling seasoned with
herbs or together with red currants etc.
as red groats (refer to the individual recipes).

79

BUCKWHEAT, RICE, POTATOES, LEGUMES, ETC.

BUCKWHEAT GROATS "KASHA"

●

Ingredients:

1 cup buckwheat
1 cup water
100 g OLEOLOX
1/2 tsp aromatic salt
2 dashes Tabasco sauce
1 tblsp soya sauce

■

Preparation:

In a pot, bring the water to a boil. On a second burner melt the OLEOLOX in a frying pan and immediately add the buckwheat, preferably the coarse form. Sprinkle aromatic salt over the buckwheat. Stirring constantly with a wooden spoon, lightly roast the buckwheat (no longer than 1/2 minute). Now pour the buckwheat into the boiling water. Either remove the pot from the element immediately or turn off the heat. The buckwheat will continue to swell, absorbing all the water. It remains nicely granular until served. Finally, top with soya sauce and Tabasco.

80

BUCKWHEAT, RICE, POTATOES, LEGUMES, ETC.

BUCKWHEAT, GRANULAR

•

Ingredients:

1 cup buckwheat
1/2 cup OLEOLOX
2 cups water
Aromatic salt

■

Preparation:

In a pot, bring the water to a boil. In a frying pan,
(which preferably has been seasoned by being heated
empty, as prescribed for the Fissler Bratfixpan) melt 1/4
pound OLEOLOX and immediately and before the fat
is heated, add the dry buckwheat groats or the whole
buckwheat kernel. Heat briefly over low flame (at most
3 minutes), until all of the fat has been absorbed by the
buckwheat. Now pour the buckwheat into the boiling
water and stir well. All the water will be absorbed by
the buckwheat. On very low heat, let it stand another
15-30 minutes to swell, depending on whether the
buckwheat groats or the whole buckwheat kernels have
been used.
This granular form of buckwheat, which is already very
tasty simply seasoned with a little salt, is generally
preferred over the porridge. The granular buckwheat
may be served both as a companion to vegetables and
in combination with raw applesauce
(as prepared in No.146).

81

BUCKWHEAT, RICE, POTATOES, LEGUMES, ETC.

BUCKWHEAT AS SOUP

●

Ingredients:

1 cup buckwheat groats
3 cups water
Vegetable stock any kind
(especially the broth from
1/2 lb fresh mushrooms)
Salt
Soya sauce
Yeast flakes or yeast extract
1/4 lb. OLEOLOX

■

Preparation:

Over a very low flame, heat 1 cup buckwheat groats in 3 cups water for 1 hour and to let it swell. The buckwheat is made into a soup by adding the various vegetable broths from leek, spinach, green beans, celery or a mixture of vegetables. For the amounts indicated, flavor with 2 tablespoons soya sauce and/or 1 tablespoon yeast flakes, 3 cm yeast extract from the tube, 1/2 teaspoon paprika, and finally OLEOLOX. By stirring and possibly adding some yeast flakes, the fat must be completely absorbed so that it does not float on top of the soup. This buckwheat soup is very well tolerated by the unwell. It should be served on its own for dinner and therefore must be flavored differently on a daily basis by changing the vegetable broths and the seasonings.

82

BUCKWHEAT, RICE, POTATOES, LEGUMES, ETC

BUCKWHEAT, SAVORY, WITH SHREDDED COCONUT

•

Ingredients:

2 cups buckwheat groats
2 cups water
1 cup shredded coconut
100 g OLEOLOX
1/2 tsp curry

1/2 tsp white pepper
1/4 tsp black pepper
1/4 tsp cayenne pepper
1 onion
5 garlic cloves
2 tblsp soya sauce

■

Preparation:

Prepare the coconut milk by blending 1 cup shredded coconut (or flesh form a fresh coconut) with 2 cups water (use shredded coconut that is packed in cellophane because the loose kind is very often rancid). Melt the OLEOLOX in a preheated pan, adding half of garlic finely cut and the finely chopped onions. Add the seasonings. Lastly, add 2 tablespoons soya sauce and the second half of the garlic, crushed.

Add the buckwheat groats to the fat, stirring with a wooden spoon for about 1/2 minute, depending on the coarseness of the groats. The coarse buckwheat can be roasted up to a minute. Now add the coconut milk to the buckwheat, mix well and let the buckwheat swell for a short time either over a very low flame or with the electric element turned off. This spicy buckwheat dish is very enjoyable as a side dish to vegetables or with a salad.

83

BUCKWHEAT, RICE, POTATOES, LEGUMES, ETC.

SAUERKRAUT SOUP, RUSSIAN STYLE

•

Ingredients:

250 g Sauerkraut
1/2 liter water
1 tsp whole caraway
1/2 tsp ground caraway
250 g whole buckwheat
1 tsp paprika
1/2 tsp aromatic salt
125 g OLEOLOX

■

Preparation:

Bringing the water to a boil, add the chopped sauerkraut. Before the sauerkraut cooks too long, immediately melt the fat in a preheated frying pan. Add paprika, salt, caraway and the whole buckwheat to the fat. Saute this a few seconds and then put mixture into the boiling sauerkraut. Depending on how much water has evaporated while boiling, add enough water to make a soup. This should be served very soon, so that the buckwheat is still whole but tender. Derived from a Russian recipe, this soup is more pleasing to our taste buds than we would expect. It is also refreshing and easily digested even by the unwell.

84

BUCKWHEAT, RICE, POTATOES, LEGUMES, ETC

RED GROATS MADE WITH BUCKWHEAT

•

Ingredients:

1 cup buckwheat groats
3 cup water
1 tsp honey
1 cup black currants
1 cup red currants

■

Preparation:

The buckwheat is cooked as described in No.78, by letting it swell in water over low heat until it forms a firm porridge. Adding the fresh berries to this hot porridge, mix well, then place in a pre-cooled dish, cup or small china bowl, and set in a cold place. This groats-berries combination is delicious as red groats.
Variations:
A combination of grape and currant juice
may be used in place of water.
Side dishes:
The Quark/Flax Seed Oil creams as described in
No. 1-15, or under "Desserts", can be used
as a sauce for this red groats dish.
The recipes flavored with vanilla, wine, kirsh, plum
brandy or vodka, are also very suitable.

85

BUCKWHEAT, RICE, POTATOES, LEGUMES, ETC

ROMANIAN SOUP

•

Ingredients:

125 g soya flour
125 g whole wheat flour
125 g onions
2 tblsp OLEOLOX
2 tsp paprika
1/2 tsp aromatic salt
1 l. water (approx.)
2 tblsp Flax Seed Oil

∎

Preparation:

Make a smooth but firm dough with the soya
and wheat flours by gradually adding a little
water. In a preheated, fairly deep pan, melt the
OLOELOX and add onions. Stirring constantly,
add the entire dough to the pan in the form of
grated flakes. After braising this briefly, add 1/2
liter water, 1 tsp paprika and salt. Bring to a brief
boil to cook the flakes, but do not overcook to
prevent falling apart. The soup may be diluted
with a little water or served as a fairly thick and
richly spiced soup.
Very suitable for the unwell.

86

BUCKWHEAT, RICE, POTATOES, LEGUMES, ETC

TOMATO-RICE,
EAST INDIAN STYLE I

●

Ingredients:

2 cups whole rice
4 cups water
1 cup shredded coconut
1 large onion
5 Tabasco dashes
1 pinch black pepper
1 pinch cayenne pepper
1 lb. tomatoes
1 tblsp curry
3 tblsp OLEOLOX
3 tblsp Flax Seed Oil
1 tblsp pumpkin seed oil
Salt

■

Preparation:

Adding the rice to cold water, bring to a gentle boil. Reduce heat so that the rice softens more through swelling than actually boiling. While the rice is still quite granular but almost done, add the shredded coconut, finely chopped onions, pepper, chopped tomatoes and the curry to the rice. Let it boil at most another 5-10 minutes. Add the OLEOLOX and oil just before serving, mix well and serve.

87

BUCKWHEAT, RICE, POTATOES, LEGUMES, ETC

TOMATO-RICE,
EAST INDIAN STYLE II

●

Ingredients:

Same as No.86 adding
1/2 lb cheese, such as:
Emmentaler or Sbrinz
or Gouda or herb-cheese

■

Preparation:

Prepare the tomato-rice as in No. 86. Lastly, sprinkle 1/2 lb. Emmentaler cheese, Sbrinz or add Gouda cheese over the rice. If one is using the Geska herb-cheese, use only half the amount.

88

TOMATO-RICE
EAST INDIAN STYLE III

●

Ingredients:

Same as in No. 86
adding
1/4 lb shredded coconut

■

Preparation:

Prepare the tomato-rice as in No. 86. Lastly, sprinkle 1/4 lb shredded coconut over the rice and serve.

89

BUCKWHEAT, RICE, POTATOES, LEGUMES, ETC

DALMATIAN RICE

●

Ingredients:

1 cup rice
2 cups water
2 garlic cloves
2 tblsp OLEOLOX
1/2 tsp aromatic salt
1 tsp paprika
1/2 tsp pepper

■

Preparation:

In a separate pot, bring the water to a boil. Melt OLEOLOX in a frying pan, immediately adding the garlic cloves, salt, pepper, paprika and finally the rice. Stirring constantly with a wooden spoon, heat the rice for at most 1/2 minute. Now place the rice in boiling water. The rice does not take long to cook, so the heating element can be turned off and the rice left to swell.

This Dalmatian rice can easily be diluted with water to make a soup. In this case, it is good to add 2-3 tablespoons of milk to round off the flavor.

90

BUCKWHEAT, RICE, POTATOES, LEGUMES, ETC

SWEET RICE

●

Ingredients:

1 cup rice
1 cup milk
2 cups water
1 tblsp honey
3 tblsp OLEOLOX
50 g hazelnuts

■

Preparation:

The rice is cooked over very low heat. Honey is added only at the end. When the rice is done, melt the OLEOLOX in a frying pan and add the finely ground hazelnuts. Heat slightly, stirring constantly with a wooden spoon. Immediately add the cooked rice to the frying pan. If the rice is too dry, a cup of milk can be gradually added. This dish can be served as a milky soup or a dry rice dish.

91

BUCKWHEAT, RICE, POTATOES, LEGUMES, ETC

LENTIL SOUP

●

Ingredients:

1/2 lb. lentils
2 medium potatoes
1 leek stalk
1 tsp paprika
1 pinch cayenne pepper
1/4 lb. OLEOLOX

■

Preparation:

Wash the lentils. Start them in cold water, then cook over low heat until done. Add potatoes which have been washed, peeled and cut into small pieces and the leek that has been cut into 3 or 4 pieces. Lastly, flavor with OLEOLOX, paprika, pepper and possibly yeast extract (from a tube). Other variations are possible; ie: chopped onion or chopped onion with garlic, lightly browned in OLEOLOX. Add this to the lentil soup just before serving.

As simple as these cooking directions may seem, they are nevertheless very important. Experience has shown that many people are unable to flavor even the simplest dishes if asked to eliminate meat, the customary sausages, or bacon.

92/93

BUCKWHEAT, RICE, POTATOES, LEGUMES, ETC

PEA SOUP
BEAN SOUP

●

Ingredients:

Same as No. 91
except replacing lentils
by other legumes.

■

Preparation:

Follow instructions for the lentil soup in No. 91.
Both dishes allow for excellent flavor variations,
even without using meat, sausage or bacon.
White beans are good with plenty of sweet
paprika and cayenne pepper.
In pea soup, 2-3 cm of yeast extract is
recommended.

91

94

BUCKWHEAT, RICE, POTATOES, LEGUMES, ETC

POTATOES

•

Ingredients:

1 lb. potatoes
100 g almonds
1 cup whole milk

(optional
2 tblsp OLEOLOX
100 g parsley)

■

Preparation:

As often as possible, potatoes should be boiled
unpeeled. You can improve them by tossing them
with OLEOLOX and plenty of
finely chopped parsley.

Another nice variation includes:
peeling the hot, cooked potatoes and tossing
them in almond milk just before serving. For the
almond milk, puree the almonds in 1 cup of
milk. If there is too much liquid, let it evaporate
over low heat.

95

BUCKWHEAT, RICE, POTATOES, LEGUMES, ETC

MACEDONIAN POTATO SOUP

●

Ingredients:

1 lb. potatoes
1 lb. onions
1 cup milk
1/4 lb. OLEOLOX
1 tsp pepper
1/2 tsp aromatic salt

■

Preparation:

Unpeeled potatoes are boiled with chopped onions. The water should barely cover them. If you are not using a pressure cooker, the potatoes will need 20 minutes to cook. Drain the cooking water into a second container. Peel and mash the potatoes with the onions. Then add the cooking water again, along with a teaspoon of pepper, the OLEOLOX and 1 cup milk. Stir well and serve this potato soup. Chopped parsley may be sprinkled over top, but the natural flavor of this potato soup is also good.

96

BUCKWHEAT, RICE, POTATOES, LEGUMES, ETC

MARITZA SOUP

•

Ingredients:

3 carrots
3 parsley roots
1 leek stalk
2 raw potatoes
1 small celery root
1/2 cup Flax Seed Oil
2 tblsp OLEOLOX
100 g parsley
1/2 lemon

■

Preparation:

Peel the carrots, the roots of parsley and celery, and in this case, the potatoes. Cut into thin sticks or grate coarsely. Also cut the leek into thin slices. Melt the OLEOLOX in a fairly deep, preheated frying pan, adding all the vegetables, potatoes, aromatic salt and a dash of pepper. Heat briefly - at most 1/2 minute. Add a half cup of Flax Seed Oil to the vegetables and top up with 1/2 litre water. Lastly, sprinkle with finely chopped parsley, a few drops lemon juice and serve immediately as a fairly thick soup. The vegetables should not be overcooked since the vegetables and potatoes have already been cooked enough in the hot fat and are soft enough after the water is added. It is important here that the potatoes not be cut into too thick pieces and are best coarsely grated. This soup is delicious, easily digested and slightly diuretic, which is important for the unwell.

BUCKWHEAT, RICE, POTATOES, LEGUMES, ETC

POTATOES WITH GARLIC

•

Ingredients:

1 lb. boiled potatoes
125 g OLEOLOX
3 garlic cloves
1/2 tsp aromatic salt
2 tblsp milk or
condensed milk

■

Preparation:

Peel the boiled potatoes and cut into small
pieces. Melt the OLEOLOX in a preheated
frying pan, adding the pressed garlic. Heat only
very briefly, not beyond lightly browning the
garlic. Immediately add the cut potato to the fat.
Season with aromatic salt, and lastly, add 2 tablespoons milk to the hot mass. After mixing well, it
should be served as soon as possible.
This dish is an excellent side dish for a vegetable
which is not too strongly seasoned (ie: fennel, a
cucumber dish, lightly seasoned spinach, etc.).
It is also a good side dish with salads.

VEGETABLES

When choosing vegetables, only fresh, undamaged products must be selected. Organic vegetables should preferably be chosen over chemically enhanced ones.

Vegetables should not be overcooked. Some vegetables soften very quickly, making them easy to chew, retaining their aroma and valuable nutrients. Overcooked vegetables loose much of their flavor and nutritional value. Not every type of vegetable need be prepared as pulp. Spinach, savoy cabbage and leeks are also tastier when they are served intact.

The simple traditional method of boiling vegetables in water is better than the modern method of "sauteeing in oil", a process during which the fat is altered and becomes harmful and difficult to digest, the vegetables often overheated.

There is no objection to the pressure cooker. The cooking time should only be as long as is necessary for the vegetables to be done. Preparation can continue after they are cooked. Vegetables can be mixed in the serving dish with melted OLEOLOX and various types of peppers, a crushed garlic clove and where appropriate, finely chopped onions, chives, parsley, fresh garden herbs, (ie: marjoram, dill, estragon or a few maggie leaves), as well as soya sauce according to taste. The intensity of the spices can be moderated by adding a few tablespoons of milk. The vegetables that have just been removed from the pressure cooker or the vegetable water are tossed with the seasoning/OLEOLOX mixture.

(continued)

Adding a few spoonfuls of the resulting fatty, savory vegetable juice to the leftover water, that the veggies are boiled in makes a delicious broth. Enhance the flavor and nutritional value by adding a few tablespoons of yeast flakes.

A sprinkling of grated cheese offers an interesting addition to the vegetable dish or to vegetable broths served in a cup, and makes different variations possible.

It is especially important for the unwell that several types of vegetables be served or that vegetables such as nettles or spinach be given two different flavors (ie: one with nutmeg and another flavored with yeast).

Overcooked veggies (ie: if pot is thoughtlessly left on the stove) lose much of their flavor and nutritional value.

98

VEGETABLES

SPINACH
TWO DIFFERENT STYLES

●

Ingredients:

1 lb. spinach
1 tsp aromatic salt
2 tblsp soya sauce
1 tblsp yeast flakes
Nutmeg
2 tblsp OLEOLOX

■

Preparation:

Wash the spinach; steam in a little water, then remove from water and either puree or finely chop. Divide the spinach into equal halves. To one half, add 2 tablespoons soya sauce, plenty of powdered or freshly grated nutmeg and 1 tablespoon OLEOLOX. Mix well and serve. The other half of the spinach is combined with the aromatic salt and the yeast. Serving both dishes side by side stimulates the appetite of an ill person and is very tasty, for example, with buckwheat.

99

VEGETABLES

CLEAR VEGETABLE BROTH

•

Ingredients:

Vegetable broth of any kind
5 garlic cloves
75 g OLEOLOX
1/2 tsp aromatic salt
1 tblsp parsley

2 tblsp yeast flakes
A pinch white pepper
A pinch cayenne pepper
1 tblsp soya sauce
1 tsp marjoram

Preparation:

Melt the fat in a preheated casserole. Add pressed garlic cloves to the warm fat, add pepper, paprika and yeast flakes, while stirring in the salt. Depending on the desired flavor, cooking water of different kinds of vegetables can be added. Water from spinach, green beans and other vegetables is very suitable. Now add the marjoram, bring to a quick boil and serve in soup cups as a clear broth before the meal. The savory flavor can be moderated by adding 1-2 tablespoons of condensed milk.

This broth can also be used in making soups.
(a) by adding granual/cooked buckweat (No. 79 or 80)
(b) in which well-cooked rice is used.
(c) by giving small noodles or other additions to the broth.
(d) Flax Seed dumplings (No. 100) are a superior addition.

VEGETABLES

***

FLAX SEED DUMPLINGS
(AS AN ADDITION TO CLEAR SOUPS)

•

Ingredients:

1 cup Flax Seed
1 cup seasoned broth

■

Preparation:

Put the intact, high quality Flax Seed in the
blender. Add the well-seasoned, concentrated
broth (see No. 99). This broth should be quite
concentrated, prepared by adding perhaps only
1/2 litre of vegetable stock to the herbs and
spices in No. 99. Blend the Flax Seed into a
smooth mass, pour into a cup and refrigerate.
This mixture takes 1/2 hour to solidify. Spoon
little dumplings, the size of a quarter into the hot
broth. This clear vegetable broth with Flax Seed
dumplings is loved by the unwell, stimulates the
appetite and is extremely easy to digest.

101

VEGETABLES

BRUSSEL SPROUTS I
WITH MARJORAM

●

Ingredients:

1 lb. Brussels sprouts
2 tblsp soya sauce
1 tblsp marjoram
2 tblsp OLEOLOX

■

Preparation:

The washed and cut brussel sprouts are boiled in
water until tender (10 minutes should suffice).
Pour off the water, now adding OLEOLOX, marjoram and soya sauce to the hot pot. Mix well and
serve immediately. These brussel sprouts, richly
seasoned on the outside but bland on the inside
(being cooked without salt), are an interesting and
tasty addition to a vegetable platter.

102

VEGETABLES

BRUSSEL SPROUTS II

•

Ingredients:

1 lb. Brussel sprouts
125 g OLEOLOX
2 tblsp soya sauce
1 cm yeast extract (from tube)
A pinch white pepper
A pinch cayenne pepper

■

Preparation:

Wash the brussel sprouts as usual and either leave them whole or cut in half. Boil them in a little water or in the pressure cooker. Remove them from the cooking water and mix with OLEOLOX, soya sauce, yeast extract, pepper and season with a little aromatic salt if desired. The combination of brussel sprouts with OLEOLOX is especially good since the latter brings out the individual aroma of the specific vegetables.

VEGETABLES

ONION SOUP
SWISS STYLE

●

Ingredients:

1 lb. onions
1/2 lb. rolled oats
Salt
Pepper
Paprika
125 g OLEOLOX

■

Preparation:

The onions are cooked in the OLEOLOX until
they become glassy (ie. heated just until they
begin to brown). To this, add one litre of water.
Bring to a boil, then add 1/2 lb. rolled oats to the
boiling water. Cook this briefly, stirring
constantly. Pass the whole mixture through a
sieve or puree it in a blender. Add more water
until the soup is creamy. Flavor with salt, pepper
and paprika, but you can also wait to sprinkle
with the red paprika after filling the plates. This
soup is tastier than one might expect.

VEGETABLES

ARTICHOKES
WITH GARLIC SAUCE I

●

Ingredients:

3 artichokes	*Salt*
6 garlic cloves	*Peppers*
1/4 litre Flax Seed Oil	*125 g Quark (optional)*
Juice of 1 lemon	*3 tblsp milk (optional)*

■

Preparation:

Cut off the hard parts of the stem and the leafy tips of the artichokes. Boil them in salt water until the outer leaves come off when they are lightly pulled. Take the artichokes from the salt water and put them into a bowl. The leaves that fall off are put into little bowls.

While the artichokes are boiling, prepare
this simple, cold sauce:
Add pressed garlic cloves to oil. Then add the juice of 1 lemon and a little salt. This oil-sauce can be used to brush the artichoke leaves before they are eaten, together with the artichoke heart.

The following is a very nice combination:
Add 125 g Quark and 3 tablespoons milk to this garlic oil dip, and mix well. This type of garlic dip is very pleasing together with the artichoke leaves
and the artichoke heart.
You can serve various vegetables that have simply been boiled in salt water; eg. beans, carrots, cubed celery root, peppers, asparagus, together with the artichokes and the above-mentioned sauce.

105

VEGETABLES

ARTICHOKE
WITH QUARK/FLAX SEED OIL MAYONNAISE II

●

Ingredients:

5 artichokes
250 g Quark
150 g Flax Seed Oil
75 g milk
1 tblsp mustard
3 pickles
Salt
1 tblsp parsley or chives, or marjoram

■

Preparation:

After removing the hard parts of the stems and the leafy tips, boil the artichokes in salt water. A garlic clove can be added to the water. While the artichokes are cooking (until an outer leaf can be pulled off easily), prepare the following mayonnaise:

In a blender, combine the Flax Seed Oil, milk, mustard, salt & quark. Lastly, add the dill pickles and puree everything until smooth. Finally, add parsley or chives to the mayonnaise. The parsley can be simply pureed along with the mayonnaise, but the chives are best added finely chopped.

This mayonnaise is served as a sauce with the piping hot artichokes. Every separated leaf can be eaten with a little mayonnaise. Best of course, is the artichoke heart, richly covered with this mayonnaise. This dish is superb in a diet for the unwell, having a beneficial effect on both the liver and the fat metabolism.

106

VEGETABLES

Comfrey Root
with Mayonnaise

●

Ingredients:

1 lb. comfrey root
A little lemon juice
100 g Quark
3 tblsp Flax Seed Oil
3 tblsp milk
Salt
Ginger

■

Preparation:

Pour boiling water over the comfrey roots. They can now be easily peeled with a paring knife. Immediately put the peeled comfrey roots into water which contains a little lemon juice or apple cider vinegar (to prevent them from turning brown). Cook the roots in hot water or in a pressure cooker.
Serve the hot roots with the following mayonnaise: Combine milk, Flax Seed Oil and Quark in a blender. Then add lemon juice. Lastly, add a good pinch of ginger and a little salt to the mayonnaise, pour it into prewarmed bowls and serve with the hot comfrey roots.

VEGETABLES

ASPARAGUS WITH MAYONNAISE
HOT OR COLD

●

Ingredients: (For 4 persons)

2 lb. asparagus
150 g Flax Seed Oil
75 g milk
250 g Quark
5 dill pickles
1 tsp mustard
1/2 banana
Salt

■

Preparation:

Prepare the asparagus as usual: tie into bundles
with a thread and boil them in salted water.
While the asparagus is boiling,
prepare the following mayonnaise:
First thoroughly blend the Flax Seed Oil, milk,
mustard and a pinch of salt. Gradually add the Quark
and mix this until smooth. Lastly, blend in at most 1/2
banana. This sauce is served with the hot asparagus.
Holding the ends of the asparagus, draw the tips
through the mayonnaise. Eat them hot. The taste is
supreme! This asparagus dish makes a satisfying meal
and is highly recommended for patients who have
difficulty passing water.

108

VEGETABLES

SAUERKRAUT
WITH PEPPERS

•

Ingredients:

2 nice peppers, either green or red
250 g sauerkraut
4 heaping tblsp yeast flakes
125 g OLEOLOX
4 tblsp pumpkin seed oil
Salt
1 tblsp soya sauce

■

Preparation:

Remove stem and seeds from the peppers_quarter them
and cut in half again crosswise. Melt the OLEOLOX in
a preheated frying pan. Immediately add the cut peppers,
covering them with a layer of sauerkraut and heat until
hot. Sprinkle the sauerkraut with 4 tablespoons yeast
flakes. While it is being heated, gradually add the pumpkin
seed oil, so that the OLEOLOX won't be overheated.
With a spatula, carefully fold the mixture so that the
layers are left relatively intact. Add a few dashes of soya
sauce and serve with hot potatoes, rice or buckwheat.
This dish can also be eaten without these side dishes
because it has a high content of yeast flakes.

VEGETABLES

SAUERKRAUT
SIMPLE STYLE

●

Ingredients:

125 g OLEOLOX
1 tblsp pumpkin seed oil
250 g sauerkraut
1 onion
Yeast extract
Aromatic salt

■

Preparation:

Melt the OLEOLOX in a preheated frying pan
and heat the onion rings until they begin to
brown. Immediately add the sauerkraut. Mix
well, add 2 cm of yeast extract from the tube and
heat until hot. The sauerkraut may be cut a little
smaller. While still on the heating element, mix
in a tablespoon of pumpkin seed oil. Some onion
rings can be used to garnish at the end. Serve as a
side dish to mashed potatoes.

VEGETABLES

KALE

•

Ingredients:

1 lb. kale
125 g OLEOLOX
3 garlic cloves
1 small onion
Nutmeg
Black, white, and
cayenne pepper
1 tblsp condensed milk
1 tblsp soya sauce

■

Preparation:

Wash the kale, remove the stems and then boil in a layered pressure cooker (15 min. is enough). In the meantime, melt the OLEOLOX in a preheated frying pan. Immediately add the finely chopped onions and pressed garlic cloves. Heat on low heat only until the onions turn glassy. The garlic should also only be heated to browning. Pour this fat into a pre-warmed serving dish, and mix it with plenty of the three kinds of pepper and 1 tbsp soya sauce. Now mix the hot vegetable with the seasoned fat in the bowl. The kale is cut a little finer but not minced. Kale tastes better like this than with "Bratwurst".

VEGETABLES

LEEKS

•

Ingredients:
(For 4 persons)

5-6 medium leeks
3 tblsp OLEOLOX
3 tblsp soya sauce

■

Preparation:

Remove the wilted parts of the leeks and wash the upper part of the yellow zone very thoroughly, if necessary, by slicing open the upper end of the solid stem. Cover the bottom of a dish with the green leaves and layer the tender yellow-white parts over them, lengthwise. Cover with water and cook until done, without adding salt. When the water has almost completely evaporated (if need be, one may have to pour off the extra liquid), pour OLEOLOX and soya sauce over this vegetable and serve immediately. The broth is delicious as a drink when it is flavored with paprika, OLEOLOX and soya sauce. Where an abundance of fat is used (if that is appropriate for the patient), the fat should be bound by adding a tablespoon of yeast flakes so that the fat is not visible. The addition of protein in the form of yeast flakes is very healthy and is considered more than just a flavoring agent.

VEGETABLES

GREEN BEENS

•

Ingredients:

1 lb. green beans
3 tblsp OLEOLOX
2 garlic cloves
Savory
1 tblsp soya sauce
1/2 tsp aromatic salt

∎

Preparation:

Wash, de-string the beans and break them into
pieces. Steam the beans in a little water together
with a little savory and a whole garlic clove. In a
bowl, prepare a sauce made of melted OLEOLOX, a
crushed garlic clove, 1 tablespoon of soya sauce, salt
and perhaps also paprika. Add the cooked beans to
the sauce, mix well and serve.
The vegetable stock that is left over can be prepared
as a drink by adding 1 tablespoon of the sauce that
was prepared for the vegetable. Additional variations
are possible by adding
1 tablespoon yeast flakes, tomato paste,
pritamin or grated cheese.

VEGETABLES

FENNEL

•

Ingredients:
(Use 1 fennel tuber per person)

4 fennel tubers
A handful grated cheese
4 tblsp OLEOLOX
1 garlic clove
1 tblsp soya sauce

■

Preparation:

Remove the hard stem from the fennel tubers. Slice them in half lengthwise and lay them flat in a dish or pan. Boil the vegetable in very little water. Savory can be added to the cooking water.
While the vegetable is boiling, melt the OLEOLOX, add a crushed garlic clove, mix, remove from heat and add 1 tablespoon soya sauce. This sauce is poured over the fennel tubers when they are cooked (if the cooking water in the dish has not completely evaporated, pour it off and use it as vegetable broth). After covering the nicely arranged fennel tubers with the sauce, top with a handful of grated cheese. You can put them back in the oven for a few minutes, but not for too long because heating quickly reduces the digestibility of this dish.

VEGETABLES

SPINACH I

•

Ingredients:

1 lb. spinach
2 garlic cloves
Nutmeg
Black pepper
White pepper
Salt
4 tblsp OLEOLOX

■

Preparation:

Remove only the very coarse parts of the stems.
Spread the leaves out in a steamer with a wire insert.
Pour one cup water in the pot, cover and steam until
done (at most 10 minutes). The leaves should not be
overcooked and should retain their green color.
Meanwhile, melt the OLEOLOX in another pan, add
1-2 crushed garlic cloves and pour the warmed fat
into a dish. Add a pinch of black, white or red
pepper, a little freshly grated nutmeg (possibly extra
powdered nutmeg) and salt to taste. Mix the spinach
leaves with this spicy sauce.
The spinach was boiled without salt. The spinach can
be cut up quickly by cross-hatching with a knife in
the serving dish. Most people prefer it served in this
manner rather than in the pureed form.

115

VEGETABLES

SPINACH II

●

Ingredients:

1 lb. spinach
2-3 large onions
2 tblsp soya sauce
3 tblsp OLEOLOX
A handful grated cheese

■

Preparation:

Wash the spinach and boil as described in Spinach I, using a wire insert. Unsalted water ensures that the spinach is not overcooked. When partially cooked, lay the coarsely cut onions over it, cover with soya sauce, re-cover and cook for a few more minutes. With a broad spatula, fold the vegetable layer in half, so that the onions are now "sandwiched." Place this on an oblong platter and sprinkle with a handful of cheese. Before serving, pour the melted OLEOLOX over the top.

Flavor the vegetable water with a little salt, yeast flakes or yeast extract and soya sauce. Serve as a drink flavored with a little OLEOLOX.

116

VEGETABLES

GREEN CABBAGE
EAST INDIAN STYLE

●

Ingredients:

1 small green cabbage
1 cup Flax Seed Oil
1 onion
2 garlic cloves
Hot peppers or a pinch of
*Cayenne Pepper**
1 tsp curry
1-2 tblsp coconut flakes
2 tblsp OLEOLOX

■

Preparation:

Remove the stem and finely shred the cabbage. Boil for maximum 10 minutes in lightly salted water. In a separate dish, melt the OLEOLOX and heat the finely chopped onions, hot peppers or cayenne pepper and curry until the onions turn glassy. Add the coconut flakes, Flax Seed Oil, crushed garlic cloves and stir well with a wooden spoon. After straining the cabbage through a sieve, put it into the pan with the fat mixture, mix well and serve right away.

* "Capsicum annum" is the Latin name for a type of pepper that belongs to the "paprika" family. This "red pepper" is not the same as the spice that is normally sold under the label "paprika". The red Cayenne Pepper is medically of greater value and is significantly stronger. It's also known as "Spanish Pepper" or "Indian Pepper" (it is an ingredient in various kinds of curry). In East Indian cookbooks and also in English recipes, it is often used under the name "chilly-peppers".

117

VEGETABLES

STINGING NETTLES
BROTH

●

Ingredients:

Nettles
Yeast flakes
Soya sauce
OLEOLOX
Salt

Paprika
(To improve the flavor,
you can add
1 tablespoon condensed
milk)

■

Preparation:

Use only the very young shoots of the nettles or break off only the last 5-10 cm of the tender young branches (at the tips of the older plants in the summer)- do *not use the brown leaves.* You may have to put a little salt in the water to remove small insects, etc. This will fill a tall pot (30 cm or 12 in.) to the brim. Cover the bottom with 10 cm water, add a teaspoon of aromatic salt (and ocasional onion - see No. 119) and cook until done (10-15 min.). Remove from the water. The nettles can be prepared using various recipes (eg: No. 118, 119, 120 or 114, 115).

The broth is as important as the nettles, especially when it is prepared in a concentrated rather than watery form.

The broth is prepared as follows:

To 1 litre of broth, add 3-4 tblsp yeast flakes, 3-4 tblsp OLEOLOX, 1 tblsp soya sauce, a pinch of paprika and possibly 1 tblsp milk. This broth is tasty and beneficial for the unwell, as it acts as a diuretic.

VEGETABLES

NETTLES
WITH SOYA SAUCE

●

Ingredients:

A shopping bag full of nettles
2 Tblsp soya flour
125 g OLEOLOX
Salt
Paprika
1 garlic clove

■

Preparation:

Gather, clean, prepare and boil the nettles as described in No. 117.
In a preheated pan melt the OLEOLOX, immediately adding the crushed garlic. Add 2 tblsp of soya flour and stir, mixing it well with the fat. Add nettle broth, stirring constantly and bringing to a boil for 1-2 minutes while seasoning with salt, a little red paprika, cayenne and white pepper. Pour this hot sauce into a vegetable dish. Now add the hot nettles which have been cut by criss-crossing with a knife. Mix them with the sauce and serve immediately with potatoes, buckwheat or rice.

VEGETABLES

NETTLES
AS CLEAR VEGETABLES

•

Ingredients:

A bag full of nettles
1 large onion
1/4 lb. OLEOLOX
2 tblsp soya sauce
Salt
Pepper
Paprika
5 tblsp condensed milk

■

Preparation:

Gather, clean and prepare the nettles as described in
No. 117, adding a chopped onion to the boiling
nettles. The broth can be seasoned and served as an
appetizer, as described in No. 117.
Prepare the vegetable as follows:
In a pre-warmed bowl, mix the hot, slightly chopped
nettles with 1-2 tablespoons OLEOLOX. Add a little
grated nutmeg, a pinch of salt and a pinch of white and
black pepper. Mix well, pouring a few tablespoons of
condensed milk over the nettles and sprinkling the center with a little paprika. Make sure that you serve it hot.
This is an excellent side dish to buckwheat
(No. 78,79) or potatoes, or rice.

VEGETABLES

NETTLES
WITH YEAST FLAKES

●

Ingredients:

A bag full of nettles
4 tblsp yeast flakes
1 cup buckwheat groats
Borage
1 onion
125 g OLEOLOX
1 tblsp pumpkin seed oil
soya sauce

■

Preparation:

Gather, clean and cook the nettles as described in
No. 117. Boil 2 cups of water.
In a second pan melt the OLEOLOX, add a cup of
buckwheat groats and stir until the buckwheat has
completely absorbed the fat.
Now put the buckwheat into the boiling water.
Immediately add 4 tblsp of yeast flakes. The nettle
broth, which was cooked with the onion, is gradually
added to the buckwheat groats. Leave this to swell for
10 min. until all the liquid has been absorbed. Gently
combine the nettles and the buckwheat together in a
single dish. Lastly, mix 1 tblsp pumpkin seed oil with
1 tblsp soya sauce and pour over top. The granular
buckwheat and the vegetables should not be overmixed
and should remain intact.

121

VEGETABLES

MUSHROOM DISH

•

Ingredients:

100 g mushrooms
2 tblsp yeast flakes
3 tblsp Flax Seed flakes
2 tblsp OLEOLOX
1 tblsp pumpkin seed oil
A pinch cayenne pepper
A pinch black pepper
A pinch white pepper
Aromatic salt
1 garlic clove

■

Preparation:

Slice the mushrooms thinly and boil in a cup of water. While boiling, add a chopped garlic clove, salt and pepper and cook for 10 minutes. Now add the OLEOLOX and the oil and stir well. Add 2 tablespoons yeast flakes and the Flax Seed flakes, stir well and remove from flame. This mushroom dish is excellent as a side-dish to the vegetable platter, as a spread or with rice and buckwheat dishes. This dish is very tasty and very healthy for the patient.

DESSERTS

As I have already indicated in the first section (under "Quark/Flax Seed Oil"), this form of nutrition is a new lease on life for the ailing. It offers help for the unwell and a joy of life for the family and children. "I would never have thought that one could make such delicious goodies out of this", remarked a surprised minister's wife, who was sick herself, and living according to the "Oil Protein-Diet" while convalescing in Lauterbach.

The following recipes for serving fruit juices are important. Pure, unsweetened juices are natural medicines and are also loved by children. Healthy and sick people alike welcome the preparation of these foods as "Fruit-Foam" or "Linovita-in-Love" or "Red Coat in the Snow".

When experimenting with the preparation of these beautiful desserts, the care-giver should remember that "Quark and Flax Seed Oil" give the patient maximum energy and strength, in minimal volume.

The suggestions and recipes in this section have long been greatly appreciated by both sick and healthy people, and serve the sick person as a source of energy and regenerating nutrition. Even the sick person who can only eat small amounts of food appreciates the Quark/Flax Seed Oil preparations, with or without alcohol.

Many of the recipes that are presented here enhance the meal and are equally uplifting for the unwell as for guests.

This vital and life-giving nutriment, always fresh and beautiful and prepared in new and interesting ways, is ideal for the unwell and the whole family (see also the recipes under "ice creams").

DESERTS

LINOMEL-VESUV

●

Ingredients: (For 3 people)

200 cc grape juice
200 cc unsweetened cherry juice
100 cc Rum
8 g Agar-Agar*
3-5 tblsp Linomel

■

Preparation:

Heat grape juice to a simmer. Dissolve the Agar-Agar in
some cherry juice and stirring constantly, add it to the
simmering grape juice. Bring to a quick boil, turn off the
heat and stirring constantly, add the rum to the mixture.
Cool immediately. Fill the mass into a
pre-cooled, slender but high container and beat until
foamy, preferably with a hand blender. Spoon this into
flat dessert dishes so that almost all the foam forms a tall
pile in the middle. Sprinkle with 1-2 tablespoons of
Linomel so that almost the entire pile is covered with
Linomel except the very top - presenting a red foam cap.
Store in a cool place until served.

---

* Agar-Agar is a natural product made from sea algae. The quality can vary
slightly. Should the fruit-jelly become too firm (do a test trial), a little extra juice
may be added.

DESERTS

FRUIT-FOAM
MADE WITH CURRANT/BLUEBERRY OR CHERRY JUICE

●

Ingredients:

*250 cc grape juice
250 cc black currant juice, unsweetened
7-8 g Agar-Agar*

■

Preparation:

Heat 250 cc grape juice to simmering point. In a
cup, dissolve the Agar-Agar in some of the
currant juice. Stirring constantly, add this to the
simmering grape juice. To avoid unnecessary
heating, turn off the electric element. While
gradually adding the remaining cold fruit juice,
let it swell up briefly again until the mixture
becomes clear. Cool until it begins to gel. Now
beat the mass to a foam with a hand blender.
Immediately put it into dessert dishes (glass
dessert bowls, stemmed glasses, etc.). Serve a
vanilla Quark/Flax Seed Oil cream, such as
No. 1 or 2, with this fruit-jelly.

DESSERTS

FROTHY-WINE-SNOW

•

Ingredients:

250 cc grape juice
250 cc white wine
7-8 g Agar-Agar

■

Preparation:

Heat 250 cc of grape juice to simmering. In a cup, dissolve the Agar-Agar in some wine and stirring constantly, add it to the simmering grape juice. Turn off the heating element and while stirring gradually, add the rest of the wine. Let it cool until it begins to gel. Beat this mass to a stiff foam (with a hand blender or beater). Immediately fill dessert dishes (glass bowls, stemware, champagne glasses, etc.).

Sauce:

1. Mix 3 tablespoons of unsweetened sea buckthorn juice with a cup of grape juice and serve this as a sauce.
2. A Quark/Flax Seed Oil cream No. 1 can also be served as a sauce.

DESERTS

LINOVITA IN WINE-JELLY

•

Ingredients: (For 5 people)

250 cc grape juice
250 cc white wine
8 g Agar-Agar
6 tblsp Flax Seed Oil
4 tblsp milk
2 tsp honey
200-250 cc Quark
1/2 tsp pureVanilla powder

■

Preparation:

Heat 250 cc of grape juice until almost boiling.
Mix the Agar-Agar with some wine in a cup and
stirring constantly, add it to the simmering grape
juice. The rest of the wine is added gradually. In
about 5 minutes, this wine jelly becomes clear
and can then be divided into 5 small dessert
dishes to cool. Prepare the Quark/Flax Seed Oil
cream as described in No. 1 and 2. Distribute
this vanilla cream among the dishes of wine jelly
so that the Linovita cream sinks under the surface
of the jelly. Serve when cool.

DESERTS

FUJIYA DELIGHT

•

Ingredients: (For 3 people)

250 cc grape juice
250 cc pure currant juice
8 g Agar-Agar
Quark/Flax Seed Oil
Milk
Honey
Vanilla cream (as in No. 1)

∎

Preparation:

Heat the grape juice until almost boiling. Mix the Agar-Agar with the currant juice and stirring constantly add it to the grape juice; bring to a low boil for about 5 minutes. Set aside to cool. Divide this mass among 3 narrow, tall cups that have been rinsed in cold water. Ideally these cups should have a bottom diameter of 3-4 cm. Refrigerate to cool completely.
Prepare a Quark/Flax Seed Oil cream (as in No. 1) with milk, honey, and vanilla. Turn the red jelly upside down onto glass plates, and put the Quark/Flax Seed Oil cream on the upper half so that the top looks like the snow capped Mt.Fujiyama*.

* The beautiful hotel which has a gorgeous view of Mt. Fujiyama is named "Fujiya", hence the dessert "Fujiya Delight"

127

DESSERTS

LINOVITA-IN-LOVE
IN A FRUIT JACKET

●

Ingredients:

250 cc grape juice
250 cc cherry juice, unsweetened
8g Agar-Agar
6 tblsp Flax Seed Oil
4 tblsp milk
2 tsp honey
2 oz. Vodka or
Prune brandy or "Kirsch" or
Rum
200-250 g Quark.

■

Preparation:

For the fruit-jelly: Heat 250 cc of grape juice. Dissolve the Agar-Agar in a cup of pure cherry juice and stirring constantly, add it to the grape juice; bring to a quick boil, gradually adding the rest of the cherry juice. After the jelly has become clear, add 2 oz. Rum.
Divide this among 5 dessert dishes (glass bowls, stemware, or champagne glasses).
Prepare a Quark/Flax Seed Oil cream (See No.), using Quark, Flax Seed Oil, milk, honey and finally adding 1 or 2 oz. Vodka. When well mixed, distribute this cream among the 5 bowls of setting fruit jelly.
Refrigerate before serving.

DESSERTS

LINOVITA
IN A FRUIT JACKET

●

Ingredients: (For 5 people)

250 cc grape juice
250 cc cherry or blueberry or
currant juice, unsweetened
7-8g Agar-Agar
6 tblsp Flax Seed Oil
4 tblsp milk
2 tsp honey
200-250 Quark or Vanilla

■

Preparation:

For the fruit jelly: Heat 250 cc of grape juice until almost boiling. Dissolve the Agar-Agar in some juice and add it to the simmering grape juice, stirring constantly. Bring to a quick boil, gradually adding the rest of the fruit juice. To prevent it from boiling over, turn off the heat. It takes about 5 minutes for the mixture to clear. Divide the fruit jelly among 5 dessert dishes.
Immediately afterwards, prepare the Quark/Flax Seed Oil cream *as follows:* mix Flax Seed Oil, milk and honey, gradually add the Quark and finally 1/2 tsp pure vanilla powder. Distribute this cream evenly on the liquid-like fruit jelly. When the Quark/Flax Seed Oil cream sinks below the surface of the fruit jelly, this dessert is ready and will keep until the afternoon or evening, even when prepared earlier in the morning.

DESSERTS

KAKI FRUIT DELIGHT

•

Ingredients:

2 Kaki fruits
Quark/Flax Seed Oil
(as in recipe No. 1)
Milk
Honey

■

Preparation:

Remove the skin of the Kaki fruit. Cut 1 Kaki
fruit into small pieces and put it in a glass bowl.
Prepare the Quark/Flax Seed Oil cream as per
No. 1 or 2, finally adding the second Kaki fruit
to the blender and pureeing it with the
Quark/Flax Seed Oil cream. Pour the cream over
the fruit in the bowl. A piece of the Kaki fruit
can be used to garnish.

DESSERTS

RED JACKET IN THE SNOW

•

Ingredients:

250 cc grape juice
200 cc pure cherry
8 g Agar-Agar
50 cc Rum
Quark/Flax Seed Oil
Cream with vanilla,
(as in recipe No. 1)
Nuts

■

Preparation:

Heat 250 cc grape juice until almost boiling. Mix the Agar-Agar with some cherry juice and add it to the grape juice while stirring constantly. Bring to a quick boil and continue cooking about another 5 minutes. Finally, add rum and set aside to cool. Divide this Cherry-Rum-Jelly into 5 little bowls or stemware.

The Quark/Flax Seed Oil cream, pureed with vanilla, or with nuts, is added to the half-liquid jelly just before it sets. Put 2 heaping tablespoons of the fairly firm Quark/Flax Seed Oil cream in the middle of the partially-set jelly, into which it should sink down. You can also add so much Quark/Flax Seed Oil cream that the cherry jelly only surrounds this white mass as a red mantel.

DESERTS

LINOVITA-IN-LOVE
IN A WINE JELLY

●

Ingredients: (For 5 people)

250 cc grape juice
250 cc white wine
8 g Agar-Agar
4 tblsp milk
6 tblsp Flax Seed Oil
2 tsp honey
200-250 g Quark
2 oz Vodka or Slibowitz or prune
brandy or "Black Forest Kirsch"

■

Preparation:

Heat 250 cc grape juice until almost boiling. Mix the
Agar-Agar with a little wine and stirring constantly, add
it to the simmering grape juice. Turn off the heat
immediately and while stirring constantly, gradually
add the rest of the wine. The jelly mixture clears itself
in about 5 minutes. Divide the jelly among 5 dessert
dishes (glass bowls, stemware, champagne glasses, etc.).
Immediately afterwards, prepare the Quark/Flax Seed
Oil cream using the Flax Seed, milk, honey and Quark.
Finally, add 2 ounces of Vodka, Slibowitz,
"Kirsch" or rum to the cream.
Divide this Quark/Flax Seed Oil cream equally among
the 5 bowls of partially set, semi-liquid jelly so that the
cream partially sinks down in the middle.
Let it set completely, then serve.

DESERTS

QUARK/FLAX SEED OIL CREAM
WITH SEA BUCKTHORN FILLING

●

Ingredients: (For 5 people)

1 cup Flax Seed Oil (150 cc)
1/2 cup whole milk
3 tsp honey
250 g Quark
5 tblsp sea buckthorn, unsweetened
5 tblsp white grape juice.

■

Preparation:

Prepare the Quark/Flax Seed Oil cream as per
No. 1 with the Flax Seed Oil, milk, honey and
Quark. The cream should be quite stiffly regulated
by adding firm Quark. Divide the
cream into 5 dessert dishes.
Now mix equal amounts of unsweetened sea
buckthorn juice and white grape juice. Pour this
into the middle of the cream before it sets so that
the liquid sinks to the bottom of the cream.
The cream will firm when left to stand another
15 minutes. Serve for dessert. The sea
buckthorn/grape juice filling comes through best
when eaten, and serves as a pleasant contrast to
the mild Quark/Flax Seed Oil cream.

DESERTS

GENERAL INFORMATION
For Making Ice Cream (Frozen Dishes)

The various sweet mixtures of Quark/Flax Seed Oil with either fruits or flavors such as vanilla, cinnamon, etc., can all be prepared and served as ice creams. Because of the oil content, the ice cream is beautifully smooth. The unwell patient who starts with a prior aversion to Flax Seed Oil will not even notice that they are ingesting Quark and Flax Seed Oil in this manner.

There are also many possibilities for making tasty preparations: Quark, Flax Seed Oil and milk are pureed with apple and horseradish, and frozen. Highly suitable as a side-dish when served in this form.

DESSERTS

ICE CREAM WITH FRUIT OR FRUIT-JUICES

●

Ingredients:

3 tblsp Flax Seed Oil
2 tblsp milk
1 tblsp honey
100 g Quark
3 heaping tblsp raspberries
or
3 tblsp pure cherry juice,

■

Preparation:

Mix Quark, Flax Seed Oil, milk and honey in blender (see No.1). Add either the raspberries or cherry juice. Pour the semi-liquid Flax Seed Oil cream into the ice-maker and put in the freezer compartment. This fruity ice cream is smooth and easily removed with a spoon to offer the unwell for dessert. Combining this fruit-ice with vanilla-ice is delicious.

134

DESSERTS

ICE CREAM WITH BLUEBERRIES

●

Ingredients:

3 tblsp Flax Seed Oil
2 tblsp milk
1 tblsp honey
100 g Quark
3 tblsp blueberries
1 handful walnuts

■

Preparation:

Mix the Quark, Flax Seed Oil, milk and honey
in a blender (seeNo. 1).
Puree with the blueberries. Add a handful of
walnuts and mix briefly so that the walnuts are
well chopped, but still remain granular. Pour this
cream into the ice-maker and freeze.
This mixture is exquisite.

DESERTS

ICE CREAM WITH VANILLA (VANILLA ICE CREAM)

●

Ingredients:

3 tblsp Flax Seed Oil
3 tblsp milk
1 tblsp honey
100 g Quark
1 tsp ground vanilla

■

Preparation:

Mix the Quark, Flax Seed Oil, milk and honey
in a blender; mix well with the vanilla. Pour this
into the ice-maker right away, while the cream is
still liquid, place in the freezer. This ice cream is
very smooth when frozen and can be easily
served to the unwell as dessert, especially in
combination with 2-3 differently
colored ice creams.

DESERTS

ICE CREAM WITH COCOA

●

Ingredients:

3 tblsp Flax Seed Oil
3 tblsp milk
1 tblsp honey
100 g Quark
100 g hazelnuts
2 tblsp cocoa

■

Preparation:

Mix the Quark, Flax Seed Oil, milk and honey in
a blender; add the hazelnuts, blend well, finally
adding the cocoa. Pour the whole mixture into
the ice-maker and put into freezer.
This nut-flavored mixture gives the various
aforementioned combinations the desired
dark color contrast.
These ice cream dishes are very important for the
very ill person, especially when there
is a general lack of appetite.

SAUCES AND SIDE DISHES

A good cook and experienced gourmet knows that sauces give the meal a decisive note. An exceptionally good cook even knows "that the secret of good cuisine lies in the correct choice and use of fats. Fats are to be added at the end, if possible". This is also the secret of the familiar, delicious Chinese cuisine. Fats should not be overheated. "Dead" fats rob the dish and the spices of their life essence. It is important to add the fat last, not to overheat it and furthermore, to choose the live, natural, highly unsaturated fats. Try the following experiment in your kitchen: prepare, for example, two curry sauces, using exactly the same recipe, one with margarine and the second with the Flax Seed Oil rich OLE-OLOX. Try both sauces side by side. The aroma of the curry is incomparably fuller, nicer and milder using OLE-OLOX which contains natural oil. You can even add additional Flax Seed Oil and the aroma remains invariably good. Fat is similarly essential for flavor in almost all dishes. As with fat, sauces represent the core of food preparation and should proceed with sensitivity; please use only well-preserved spices. Do not use spices and herbs that are stored in paper bags, or old remains of formerly gathered herbs that you find in a container, but rather use good herbs and spices that are stored in separated tightly sealed jars. Combine things with expert knowledge and thoughtfulness. An elegant sauce pays testimony to a refined personality. This is valid for the hot sauces as well for the salad sauces that are based on the Quark/Flax Seed Oil mayonnaise. We know that good artists are great cooks. Very stimulating are the Syrian and the Turkish combinations of various kinds of nuts with garlic, pepper and paprika, in good, oil-rich sauces. These are interesting as a sauce or as a nut side dish

(continued)

to the vegetable platter. Seasoning herbs can always be used and stored as vinaigrette in a vinegar oil mixture. If one takes the meat and the pre-made meat preparations away from the homemaker, only then will they begin to display their capabilities as cook and master of the kitchen and table. If the cook gives his/her ideas and possible combinations full range, she will be able to give the dishes her own special touch. If it is true that "The way to the heart is through the stomach", then delicious sauces have the capacity to make the homemaker beloved by all.

SAUCES AND SIDE DISHES

SYRIAN SIDE DISH I

•

Ingredients:

50 g walnuts
50 g almonds
50 g hazelnuts
50 g pine-nuts
1 tsp paprika
1/2 tsp cayenne pepper
1 medium onion
2-3 garlic cloves
2 Tblsp Flax Seed Oil
2 Tblsp OLEOLOX

■

Preparation:

Put 2 tablespoons Flax Seed Oil in a blender and gradually
add nuts, season with paprika and cayenne pepper, and
now blend. Melt the OLEOLOX in a frying pan, add
the finely chopped onions and crushed garlic cloves and
heat until they begin to brown. Stirring constantly with
a wooden spoon, add all of the nuts, oil and pepper. Stir
only a few seconds before adding a cup of water. Bring
to a quick boil, and then set aside.
This nut mixture is excellent as a side dish to vegetables,
or by adding a little more water and a little salt, as
a sauce served with either rice, buckwheat, potato or
with fresh fish dishes.

138

SAUCES AND SIDE DISHES

SYRIAN SIDE DISH II

•

Ingredients:

50 g walnuts
50 g almonds
50 g hazelnuts
50 g pine nuts
3 tblsp whole wheat bread crumbs
3-4 garlic cloves
1/2 cup (75 g) Flax Seed Oil
Juice of 1-2 lemons
Salt
2 tblsp OLEOLOX

◾

Preparation:

Mix the oil, lemon juice and nuts in a blender. Add the crushed garlic and blend again. Melt the OLEOLOX in a frying pan. Stirring constantly; add the bread crumbs, and after a few seconds (1/2 min.) add all of the nut-cream. Put this sauce into a bowl, where it can be mixed with either finely-cut endive lettuce or chicory salad. This is excellent in combination with 1/2 jar sweet & sour paprikas, using both the paprika slices and the mild vinegar.
For other variations, use dill pickles or other mixed pickles. If desired, a little apple cider vinegar can also be added. This combination is also appealing to our tastes.

139

SAUCES AND SIDE DISHES

NUT PAPRIKA SAUCE

●

Ingredients:

1/2 lb. onions
3 garlic cloves
1/2 lb. walnuts
1-2 tblsp sweet paprika
1 cup Flax Seed Oil
2 tblsp OLEOLOX
Salt
Water

(optional:)
1 tblsp yeast flakes
and / or
2 tblsp soya sauce

■

Preparation:

Put the oil and the walnuts into a blender. Melt the
OLEOLOX in a frying pan, then add the finely
chopped onions. Heat until they begin to brown, and
only then add the crushed garlic cloves and the
paprika. Finally, add the walnuts with Flax Seed Oil.
After heating this a few seconds, add enough water to
make a creamy sauce and salt to taste. Other flavor
variations are possible by adding 1 tablespoon
yeast flakes or soya sauce.

140

SAUCES AND SIDE DISHES

CURRY SAUCE

•

Ingredients:

125 g OLEOLOX
2-3 tblsp soya flour
Aromatic salt
1 tblsp soya sauce
1/2 cup Flax Seed Oil
1/2 cup milk
1 cup rice water or vegetable broth
1 heaping teaspoon
of a good East Indian curry mixture

∎

Preparation:

Melt the OLEOLOX in preheated frying pan.
Immediately add the soya flour and stir with a wooden
spoon until the soya flour is well blended but not
browned. After a few seconds, add some watery liquid
(any kind of vegetable broth or rice water, if available)
_stirring constantly. After letting it boil briefly, add a
heaping teaspoon curry, Flax Seed Oil and milk. The
sauce should have a smooth consistency and
no oil should be visible.
This sauce is very spicy and is excellent
with rice dishes or buckwheat.
The following mistake is frequently made: foods are
cooked too long, causing the aroma to dissipate and the
sauce becomes too spicy. Also, by damaging the fat
containing Flax Seed Oil, the wonderfully, rounded
aromatic flavor is compromised.

141

SAUCES AND SIDE DISHES

Horseradish Sauce

•

Ingredients:

125 g OLEOLOX
2-3 tblsp soya flour
Herb salt
1/2 cup Flax Seed Oil
1/2 cup milk
1 cup vegetable broth
2 tblsp grated horseradish

■

Preparation:

In a frying pan, prepare the soya flour as described in No. 140 (curry-sauce). Puree the horseradish with the milk (best done in a blender) and add this to the hot soya sauce. If you like the horseradish sauce on the "sharp" side, serve without heating it again.

142

SAUCES AND SIDE DISHES

FRUIT SAUCES MADE WITH PURE JUICES

•

Ingredients:

250 g cherry juice,
or currant juice,
or blueberry juice
with
250 g grape juice
3 g Agar-Agar

■

Preparation:

Heat the grape juice. Dissolve the Agar-Agar with
a little fruit juice and stirring constantly, add it to
the hot grape juice. While it is cooking, gradually
add the rest of the unsweetened juice. Set aside to
cool. This fruit sauce is suitable as a dessert to
compliment the sweet Quark/Flax Seed Oil
creams, such as Banana-Cream or Vanilla-Cream,
but it is also good with buckwheat dishes.
According to taste, one can vary the flavor when
using unsweetened cherry juice by adding
1 tablespoon Rum.

143

SAUCES AND SIDE DISHES

TOMATO SAUCE
WITH OR WITHOUT PAPRIKA

●

Ingredients:

*125 g OLEOLOX
2-3 tblsp Soya flour
Aromatic salt
1 tblsp soya sauce
1/2 cup milk
1 onion
1-2 garlic cloves
1/2 lb. tomatoes or
1 tin tomato paste*

*(optional:)
Peppers
1 tin pritamin or
Sweet & sour paprikas
from the jar)*

■

Preparation:

Prepare the soya flour sauce as described in
No. 140. Melting the OLEOLOX in a frying
pan, add the finely chopped onions. When they
begin to brown, add the soya flour and the crushed
garlic cloves. Proceed as in No. 140, using as the

143

(continued)

---

liquid 1/2 lb. tomatoes and 1/2 cup milk which have been pureed together in a blender. If fresh tomatoes are not available, substitute a tin of tomato paste from the health food store. Season with salt, soya sauce, and 1/2 teaspoon honey.

Other Variations:
A further variation of this tomato sauce is possible by adding paprika; for this use fresh, finely chopped paprikas, pritamin from the health food store or sweet & sour paprikas in a jar (from the health food store).

SAUCES AND SIDE DISHES

Soya Salad Sauces, sweet & spicy

●

Ingredients:

3 tblsp soya sauce
3 tblsp water
2 tblsp apple cider vinegar
1 Garlic clove
1 tsp honey
2 tblsp Flax Seed Oil
or
2 tblsp pumpkin seed oil
1/2 tsp ginger
1 tsp shredded coconut

■

Preparation:

a) Simply mix the soya sauce, water, vinegar and honey. Then add a pressed garlic clove. Finally, add the Flax Seed Oil or the pumpkin seed oil. This sauce is excellent with endive lettuce or chicory.

b) A very nice variation is obtained by adding shredded coconut, which has either been soaked over-night or blended with the soya sauce.

c) Another variation is obtained by adding ginger.

d) Both the above variations, the shredded coconut or the ginger can be used separately or combined. Pumpkin seed oil can also be added, if desired. You can find more uses for this soya sauce when preparing Chutneys or the various Quark/Flax Seed Oil mixtures.

SAUCES AND SIDE DISHES

TURKISH SALAD SAUCE

•

Ingredients:

75 g Walnuts
2 tblsp Quark
2 tblsp Flax Seed Oil
2 tblsp OLEOLOX
3 tblsp whole wheat bread crumbs
3 garlic cloves
Juice of 1-2 lemons
1/2 tsp honey
A pinch cayenne pepper
Finely chopped dill
Parsley
Peppermint leaves
1 tblsp milk

■

Preparation:

Blend the Quark, Flax Seed Oil, milk and lemon thoroughly. Add honey, salt, red pepper, finely chopped herbs and pressed garlic cloves. Stir everything together well and pour it into a bowl. In a frying pan, briefly warm the OLEOLOX and the bread crumbs and pour over the sauce in the bowl. Stir briefly so that the hot fat is stirred in and serve. This sauce can be served with a salad, a raw vegetable platter or combined with various kinds of grated vegetables, or with cooked vegetables.

146

SAUCES AND SIDE DISHES

RAW APPLE SAUCE
VARIOUS VARIATIONS

●

Ingredients:

1 - 1 1/2 apples
per person

A choice of:
Apple juice
Quince juice
Grape juice
Pure cherry juice

■

Preparation:

Put a cup of apple juice in the blender (pure
quince juice or cherry juice is also excellent).
While the blade is rotating and with the lid on,
add the seasoned apples. Makes much apple
sauce with relatively small amounts of juice if
you feed the apple pieces in gradually.
Raw apple sauce is easily digestible in this form,
even for the ill. It can be consumed in combination
with the buckwheat groats (No. 78 and 80) or
with potato patties made from raw potatoes
- a combination also easily digested by the unwell.

MENU SUGGESTIONS

SALAD PLATTER, VEGETABLE PLATTER WITH BUCKWHEAT

•

SALAD PLATTER

Combine endive lettuce, corn salad or cress, together with grated celery root or sliced cooked red beets. Garnish with pearl onions from a jar and grated kohlrabi. Everything is then covered with a mayonnaise (see No. 16) or with variaions suggested in No. 17-24.

VEGETABLE PLATTER WITH BUCKWHEAT

Choose 3 or 4 types of vegetable. Each vegetable is flavored with a different spice: brussel sprouts with marjoram and soya sauce; spinach is half prepared with yeast flakes and soya sauce, the other half with soya sauce and nutmeg; sliced celery root, sprinkled with plenty of grated aged Gouda cheese. Serve these together with buckwheat, which is still granular in texture (see No. 79) or prepared as a porridge (see No. 78). Heap the buckwheat in the center of the platter and arrange the vegetables in a ring around the platter (for visual appeal).

QUARK/FLAX SEED OIL AS A DESSERT

For dessert, choose one of the many Quark/Flax Seed Oil dessert recipes (eg: No. 132).

MENU SUGGESTIONS

QUARK/FLAX SEED OIL, PREPARED DIFFERENTLY

●

VEGETABLE BROTH

Heat a cup of vegetable broth, perhaps left over from
the previous day eg. spinach water, broth from leeks,
celery, green beans, etc.). To 500 cc (2 cups) broth, add
a little freshly grated nutmeg, salt, black and white
pepper, 1 heaping tablespoon OLEOLOX and 2 heaping
tablespoons yeast flakes. Serve this broth in soup cups
before the main meal.

QUARK/FLAX SEED OIL WITH POTATOES

Boil the unpeel potatoes and serve with 2 differently
flavored Quark/Flax Seed Oil mixtures.
For example, prepared as follows:
Blend 100 g Flax Seed Oil, 100 g milk, and 250 g Quark.
Pour half of this into a bowl and mix it with a teaspoon
of ground caraway and 1 tablespoon
of whole caraway seed.
Puree the second half, still in the blender
with about 200 g parsley.
Both mixtures are seasoned with a little salt and served
with the potatoes. These Quark/Flax Seed Oil preparations
can be further varied or enhanced by using the many
recipes listed under Chutneys (No. 29-36) and
Tscha-Tschi Variations (No. 37-55) or under
Quark/Flax Seed Oil Mayonnaise (No. 16-24).

FRUIT FOAM NO. 123 FOR DESSERT.

149

MENU SUGGESTIONS

NEW COMBINATIONS

•

VEGETABLE BROTH WITH RAW ADDITIONS

Save the vegetable water from the cooking of spinach and/or carrots, leeks, celery, green beans, parsley roots. Flavor 250 cc (1 cup) of this broth with 1 tablespoon OLEOLOX, 1 tablespoon soya sauce, 1 teaspoon marjoram, 1 teaspoon borage, a pinch of aromatic salt, a pinch of white and black pepper, 1/2 teaspoon red paprika, and lastly, 1 tablespoon condensed milk. This hot broth is served right away in soup cups. The broth can be combined with the following:
In a blender, puree a raw carrot or kohlrabi with some soup broth, and add this to the hot vegetable broth. This warm raw food agrees very well with the ill and is also nice for the healthy person in winter.

RICE WITH SALAD

As a main course, one can choose either a rice or a buckwheat dish, for example, No. 86-89 or 78-80 with a salad platter, perhaps No. 70 with Banana Mayonnaise or simply the buckwheat soup No. 81.

LINOMEL VESUV

For dessert, the Linomel Vesuv No. 122, Frothy Wine Snow No. 124, or Fruit Foam No. 123 are suitable as a Quark/Flax Seed Oil preparation when served with the main dish.

150

MENU SUGGESTIONS

A SMALL MEAL

•

SALAD PLATTER WITH MAYONNAISE TOGETHER WITH MASHED POTATOES

Simply serve a salad platter consisting of various salads, together with mashed potatoes or fried potatoes prepared with plenty of onions and OLEOLOX.

MENU SUGGESTIONS

SUITABLE FOR THE VERY ILL

•

GRATED APPLE WITH LINOMEL

Instead of a salad platter, the raw food consists of
a grated apple mixed with a
tablespoon of Linomel.

SOUP WITH AN ADDITION

Serve a plate of soup prepared from well-seasoned
vegetable broth, with added buckwheat groats as
in No. 81. The buckwheat groats should be
cooked separately, as a porridge or in a granular
form, as in recipes No. 78, 79, 80.

WINE CREAM

The nutritional value of the menu is enhanced
with a Quark/Flax Seed Oil cream for dessert; for
example one that is flavored with 2 tablespoons
of sweet wine, rum or cognac.

152

MENU SUGGESTIONS

A Quick Meal

●

SAUERKRAUT SOUP

Sauerkraut soup with buckwheat, prepared as in No. 83.

PINEAPPLE WITH GINGER CREAM

For dessert, a Quark/Flax Seed Oil cream flavored with cinnamon and ginger, over a slice of pineapple or combined with half a ripe pear.

MENU SUGGESTIONS

A Small Menu

●

SALAD PLATTER WITH SEASONED BUCKWHEAT

A salad platter with green lettuce, finely chopped
peppers and thinly sliced cucumber, all covered
with mayonnaise (No. 16 or No. 17-24).
In addition, serve seasoned buckwheat with
shredded coconut (see No. 82).

CHERRY BLOOD, HOT

Thereafter, serve a glass of hot, pure cherry juice
(or grape juice), flavored with cinnamon
and nutmeg.

154

MENU SUGGESTIONS

Guests Join the Table

●

A) VEGETABLE BROTH

A cup of clear vegetable broth, flavored with
yeast flakes, OLEOLOX, paprika, soya sauce
and a little pepper.

B) SALAD EXTRA FINE

In a small dish, serve on a green lettuce leaf,
celery-root salad with banana (No. 67), and
garnish with red paprika or sweet & sour tomato
paprika from a jar.

C) NUT VEGETABLE PLATTER

A vegetable platter with fennel; celery-root as a
vegetable, sprinkled with cheese or combined
with the Syrian Nut paste (No. 137); spinach
with onions; cooked carrots; savoy leaves covered
with the Turkish Sauce (No. 145); together with
whole rice, cooked to remain granular, with little salt.

D) DESSERT: LINOVITA-IN-LOVE

Linovita-In-Love for dessert
(see No. 127 and No. 131)

MENU SUGGESTIONS

MENU WITH A RUSSIAN ACCENT

•

A) VEGETABLE PULP BROTH

A well-seasoned vegetable broth with plenty of
pureed tomatoes or tomato paste, flavored with milk
or condensed milk before serving.

B) CHEESE SOUFFLE

In a small souffle form, serve a souffle consisting of
alternate layers of celery root slices and grated
cheese, with a top layer of well-seasoned, granular
buckwheat (No. 79).

C) VEGETABLE PLATTER, EXTRA SPICY

Sauerkraut prepared over peppers, sprinkled with
yeast (No. 108), together with mashed potatoes. All
this is covered with hot OLEOLOX, made aromatic
by adding a crushed garlic clove. Especially with this
sauerkraut dish, the OLEOLOX can be given a
pleasant aroma by adding a few tablespoons of yeast
flakes to the fat instead of garlic.

D) VODKA CREAM

Quark/Flax Seed Oil cream is flavored with lemon
or orange juice, possibly mixed with coarsely ground
hazelnuts and finally enhanced with Vodka.

156

MENU SUGGESTIONS

HAVING FUN WITH EAST INDIAN VARIATIONS

•

CHINESE PORCELAIN DISHES

10 small bowls, diameter 9 cm
10 small bowls, diameter 10.5 cm
10 flat Chinese bowls, diameter 10 cm
10 flat Chinese bowls, 6.5 cm
1 Soya Sauce jug, shaped like a little teapot, 5 cm high
1 Chinese teapot to make the green teas, 15 cm high
3 small bowls, diameter 16 cm
1 large bowl with a cover, diameter 25-30 cm.

THE MAIN DISH (FOR 6 PEOPLE)

A) 3 cups whole rice are boiled in 6 cups water. Add
   several drops of lemon juice to the boiling water so
   that the rice remains granular. When using whole
   rice, it is easier to produce a granular cooked rice.
   This rice is served in the large bowl with the cover,
   without added salt, without fat and without
   any seasoning.
   You can cut 4 bananas in half, lengthwise, cook them
   a little in a frying pan and arrange them over the rice.

B) For the small bowls with diameter 16 cm, prepare:
   1. Curry-Sauce No. 140
   2. Syrian Sauce I No. 137
   3. spicy, granular buckwheat No. 79

(continued)

C) Put the soya sauce in the small soya sauce jug, ready to serve.

D) **SIDE DISHES:**
Now the fun begins:

a) As with No. 29/30, prepare the **Basic Mixture for Chutney I**, made with Quark and Flax Seed Oil, the **Red Mixture Chutney II**, made with apple and red beet juice; the **Tscha-Tschi I** with walnuts and garlic, and the **Tscha-Tschi II** with the sweet addition of apple juice, grape juice or a little honey No. 37/38.

b) Side dishes for the 10 small bowls, diameter 10.5cm.
   1. Peel a tart apple and cut into 1 cm cubes.
   2. Prepare a long cucumber the same as the apple in 1.
   3. Do the same with dill pickles.
   4. Take 250 g pearl onions from a jar.
   5. Take 250 g sweet & sour paprikas from a jar and cube
   6. Pineapple, preferably fresh, cut into small pieces.
   7. Shredded coconut, fresh or dried, serve as they are.
   8. Shredded coconut, slightly roasted, dry.
   9. Pine-nuts, briefly heated.
  10. Prepare garlic oil as follows: Melt 1/2 cup OLEOLOX in a preheated pan and heat very briefly (at most 1/2 minute) with 5 pressed garlic cloves. Do not allow the garlic to brown. Immediately afterwards, add 1/2 cup Flax Seed Oil. After stirring briefly, pour this oil into the tenth bowl.

c) Into the smaller bowls (diameter 9 cm), put 1 tblsp.

(continued)

from each of the above side dishes (No. 1-9), that is-
apple, cucumber, onions, etc. In each case, put a tblsp.
of either Chutney I or Chutney II, or Tscha-Tschi I or
Tscha-Tschi II over the contents and mix. Using the
aforementioned side dishes 1-9 and the 4 ready pastes,
you can prepare 36 variations without using the tenth
side dish - the garlic oil. Adding 1tblsp of the garlic oil
to each of the 4 pastes gives you another 36 excellent
variations. In this manner you can make more variations of the 4 pastes; add them to the ten small bowls
and mix.
Into the tenth small bowl, put finely chopped dates.
Pour the Curry Sauce over this (as prepared under B),
and serve hot.

d) In the large flat bowls, put:
   1. Onion rings, raw and sliced very thin
   2. Onion rings heated in the garlic oil in dish #10
      until glassy
   3. thinly sliced almonds, (sliced with a slicing machine)
   4. Pritamin (a kind of paprika catsup)
   5. Tomato catsup
   6. Horseradish, pureed in milk, with a tablespoon of
      soya sauce over it
   7. Banana slices, piled high and sprinkled with red paprika
   8. 2 Tblsp Tscha-Tschi I with a tblsp Pritamin
   9. 2 Tblsp Tscha-Tschi II with a tblsp Pritamin
   10. 2 Tblsp Tscha-Tschi I with a knife-tip of coriander

e) Now the 10 small flat bowls are still unused.
   It is fitting to offer particularly spicy-hot, strong dishes

156

(continued)

---

in these bowls. For example, fill:
1. 3 bowls with Tscha-Tschi I,
2. 3 bowls with Tscha-Tschi II,
3. 3 bowls with Chutney II.

Now put 5 dashes of Tabasco into each of 1a, 2a, 3a, (the first bowls of 1, 2, 3);

-a knife-tip of black, white and cayenne pepper into each of 1b, 2b, 3b;
-a teaspoon of sharp paprika or Pritamin into
each of 1c, 2c, 3c.
(For 1c, 2c, and 3c you could also use 1/2 teaspoon curry powder or ginger).

In the 10th small bowl, put a tablespoon of the garlic oil (described under b, side-dish #10) with 5 dashes Tabasco, and a knife-tip of red paprika. Serve hot, preferably on a table hot-plate.

The following can also be used as side dishes:

Auberginen Salad (Eggplant Salad)
Whole peppers
Paprikas, thinly sliced
East Indians baked flat-cakes or
 in this country (Germany), you can use rye crisp
(Knaeckebrot) for the unwell person.

157

SPECIAL CIRCUMSTANCES

FOR THE INFANT (I)

•

Ingredients:

3 tblsp Linomel
3 tblsp Oat Flakes
250 cc Water

■

Preparation:

Put oat flakes into cold water and bring to a boil.
Add Linomel to the boiling gruel; bring to a
quick boil, then let stand for 10 minutes to let it
swell. Pass the whole mass through a very fine
sieve. This gruel is very healthy for the infant
and can be combined with a little milk. It is also
valuable for regulating digestion.

160

SPECIAL CIRCUMSTANCES

FOR THE INFANT (4)

•

Ingredients:

(See Recipe No. 157 - 1)
adding 50 cc Grape Juice

■

Preparation:

Prepare the gruel as in No. 157 - 1, and mix with
50 cc white or red grape juice.

161

FOR THE INFANT (5)

•

Ingredients:

(See Recipe No. 157 - 1)
adding 2 Tblsp very finely
grated Apple

■

Preparation:

Prepare the gruel as in No. 157 - 1, and combine
it with a very finely grated apple. Give to infant
to drink right away.

162

SPECIAL CIRCUMSTANCES

FOR THE VERY ILL (1)

●

Ingredients:

(See Recipe No. 157 - 1)
adding 150 cc Orange Juice
or Orange and Grape Juice mixed,
or Cherry Juice,
or red or black Currant Juice,
or Blueberry Juice,
(each mixed with an equal amount
of Grape Juice)

■

Preparation:

The Linomel-Oatmeal gruel as in No. 157 - 1,
can form the base for a wide variety of tasty
combinations that are both nutritious and easily
digested by the very ill person.
Combine 150 cc Linomel-Oatmeal gruel with
150 cc of orange juice or 150cc of grapefruit
juice or 150 cc of any of the fruit juices men-
tioned, mixed half and half with grape juice.
These unsweetened juices are very beneficial and
easily tolerated by the ill in this combination,
even when pure juice is sometimes not (also see
Desserts No. 122-136).

163

SPECIAL CIRCUMSTANCES

FOR THE VERY ILL (2)

•

Ingredients:

*(See Recipe No.157 - 1) adding
Quark/Flax Seed Oil Cream with Vanilla
as prepared in No. 1 & 2.*

■

Preparation:

Prepare the Linomel-Oatmeal gruel as in No. 157 - 1,
and put it into a soup cup. Cover the still hot gruel
with 2 tblsp of the firm and well mixed Quark/Flax
Seed Oil Vanilla Cream as in No.1 and 2, or No. 131.

164

FOR THE VERY ILL (3)

•

Ingredients

*(See Recipe No. 157 - 1)
Quark/Flax Seed Oil Cream with Lemon
1 tblsp almond puree*

■

Preparation:

Having prepared the Linomel-Oatmeal gruel as in
No. 157 - 1, finally fold in 1 tblsp of almond puree
(from the health food store). Cover with 2 tblsp of
Quark/Flax Seed Oil Lemon Cream.
Serve in a soup cup.

165

SPECIAL CIRCUMSTANCES

FOR THE VERY ILL (4)

●

Ingredients:

(See Recipe No. 157 - 1)
Quark/Flax Seed Oil
Lemon Cream
with Banana.

■

Preparation:

Prepare the Linomel-Oatmeal gruel as
in No. 157 - 1, and put into a soup cup.
The Quark/Flax Seed Oil Lemon Cream as in
No. 1 is prepared separately and spooned over top
of the gruel drink.

166

SPECIAL CIRCUMSTANCES

FOR THE VERY ILL (5)

●

Ingredients:

(See Recipe No. 157 - 1)
1-2 tblsp Red Wine
1 oz. Vodka,
or Cognac,
or Slibowitz,
or "Kirsch"
or Rum

▬
■

Preparation:

Prepare the Linomel-Oatmeal gruel as in
No. 157 - 1, lastly adding 2 tablespoons red
wine. Fill into a soup cup and cover with
2 tablespoons of a Quark/Flax Seed Oil Cream,
flavored as in No.1, No. 127 or 131. It is important
that the strong alcoholic drinks are mixed into
the Quark/Flax Seed Oil Cream separately as per
instructions in No. 127 and 131.

GUIDELINES TOWARD BETTER HEALTH

Forbidden for the Unwell

Forbidden are all fats, other than Flax Seed Oil and OLE-OLOX as well as white sugar and preparations containing white sugar. Natural sugars, as present in fruits are allowed. Strictly avoid all types of sausages and processed meats, all baked goods from the pastry shop (the combination of hydrogenated or animal fats with sugar is detrimental to good health). If one must eat out, it is very important to pay attention to the right choice of fats. If the occasion arises, it is sometimes possible to ask that dishes be prepared for you with OLEOLOX. Within the framework of the Oil-Protein Diet regimen, scrambled eggs or fried eggs prepared with bacon or lard can cause problems.

Poultry and game with added preserving agents can also exert a negative influence if ones health is unstable.

While Travelling

With the Oil-Protein Diet, you can protect yourself against harm while you are travelling by ordering fresh fish, such as trout, pike or carp.

Strictly avoid canned fish, crab and other products from the deli, because they frequently contain artificial colouring agents and harmful chemical preservatives.

While travelling, you can always care for yourself with Linomel and hot or cold milk, and/or fruit juices.

Cod-liver Oil?

The formerly esteemed cod-liver oil was beneficial on account of its poly-unsaturated fatty acids. Recently, it has become common practice to heat the cod-liver oil in high temperatures in order to give it a longer shelf-life. The consequence is that cod-liver oil which has been treated in this manner causes serious health damage. The same is true of many oils in canned fish.

A Guide out of the Maze of Nutrition Advice

One must ask what is valuable and important, what is less important, and what is hazardous to one's health because of chemical additives. One must not only ask "What is forbidden or allowed?" "Vitamins" are necessary; they are present in fresh fruits and vegetables in adequate amounts, as are the necessary "trace elements". Man cannot live from these alone!

The three basic elements of nutrition, carbohydrates, proteins and fats must under all circumstances be balanced. The basic nutrient "fat" is essential for life, as it is centrally significant for every vital function. Compared to all other nutrients, it contains by far the greatest force of energy which the body can access immediately.

"Fats" contain a life-giving principle in their wealth of Electrons.

Heart attacks, cardiac arrest,
Fatty liver with irregular gall bladder functions,
Tumor formation,
Arteriosclerosis,
Rheumatism and joint diseases,
Dry mucous membranes, also in the stomach and intestines,
are all symptomatic of the exclusion and "non-integration" of fats.

176

All living tissue says "No!" to the fats foreign to the body. This is clearly expressed through the isolation and rejection of the electrically-neutral, lame fats. These symptoms of pathological fat-metabolism cannot be corrected by the subsequent withdrawal of all fats. Eliminating harmful fats is indeed necessary, but genuine help is only possible by supplying "good fats". Water soluble fats are being highlighted here. The fats in Flax Seed ie: the electron-rich fats, which attract protein through their electrical potential, become water soluble when they combine with "good proteins", as are present in Quark. They prevent the pathological isolation of fats and promote the secretion of mucous in all organs and mucous membranes. They load the energy supply necessary for the impulses that regulate heart activity. They attract oxygen and create oxygen reserves, which are equally important to the athlete as well as the convalescent.

SPORTS DIET

A "Sports Diet" must be light. Massive doses of ingested nutrition in the stomach hamper performance. Concentrated, easily activated energy sources however, work efficiently and effectively for the sprinter as well as the marathon runner requiring more enduring breathing capabilities

With this in mind, the following is recommended:

For breakfast, the Linomel-Muesli, described in No. 1-15. It contains 300-400 calories. For fat, only OLEOLOX should be used. No heavy fats! If lean meat is desired, then it must be preservative free. Preservatives, being respiratory toxins, impair performance. The chemicals used to fatten animals also reduce the top performance levels of the athlete. The daily ration within the context of the Oil-Protein Diet contains 4000 calories. This is as important for the athlete as for someone doing hard physical work, as well as the convalescing patient. Naturally, the amounts can be reduced later.

BREAKFAST FOR YOUNG PEOPLE

"A full stomach doesn't like to study!" So goes an old Latin proverb. Everyone knows how meals that are difficult to digest impair our ability to think.

If, for their morning recess, we give children sandwiches filled with sausage and spread with indigestible fats, we will find in their blood all the symptoms associated with digestive fatigue that follow an enormous meal.

Childrens' ability to perform in school is definitely improved and the tendency to tire easily reduced, when breakfast supplies them with enough, concentrated, energy-packed and easily digested nourishment (a little fruit serves as an adequate mid-morning snack). For the main breakfast they are given the Linomel-Muesli (described in No. 1-15).

Once children have tried this breakfast, they won't want anything else any more, and rightly so!

In the Oil-Protein Diet, there are guidelines to show how the very ill person, the mostly healthy person who "can't tolerate any fat", the person doing heavy physical work, the person who does "mental work", and the athlete can avoid the burdensome effects of foods that are hard to digest. Even in our times, with the many burdens caused by our civilization, it is still possible to preserve or get back our health, as well as our ability to perform.

The FLAX OIL manufacturer in
North America
recommended by
Dr. Johanna Budwig
is
BARLEAN'S
Organic Oils

●

1-800-445-FLAX(3529)

■

made available to you by: